FEEDING THE VIKINGS

Martin F. Kilmer

AC CI PE ET LE GE

L E G A S

MARTIN F KILMER ⊕ PETER J SCOTT

WITH CONTRIBUTIONS FROM MARIE-FRANCOISE GUEDON

ORIGINAL PHOTOGRAPHY BY MARTIN F KILMER

National Library of Canada Cataloguing in Publication

Kilmer, Martin F.:

    Feeding the Vikings / Martin F. Kilmer, Peter J. Scott.

ISBN 1-894508-10-6

1. Wild plants, Edible – Newfoundland and Labrador – Pictorial works. 2. Newfoundland and Labrador – Pictorial works. I. Scott, Peter, J., 1948- II. Title.

QK98.5.C3K54 2003   581.6'32'09718022   C2002-903434-5

For further information and for orders:

LEGAS
P. O. Box 040328   3 Wood Aster Bay   2908 Dufferin Street
Brooklyn, New York   Ottawa, Ontario   Toronto, Ontario
USA 11204   K2R 1B3   M6B 3S8

http://www.legaspublishing.com

Printed and bound in Canada

To Jolene, dimidium animae meae... To our children, our grand-children, our great-grand-children, and the newly renovated bathroom...

And to all those who have made this island their home.

Acknowledgements

My first debt is to the people of Newfoundland's Great Northern Peninsula. I cannot list all who have encouraged me, given me information on local names and local uses of plants, guided me to the places where I could find and photograph the plants. There is the whole staff of the L'Anse aux Meadows Interpretation Centre – Debbie, Loretta, Clayton, Steve, Tamara, and those whose names are not surfacing. (Loretta and Steve – I haven't forgotten I owe you dinner.) The re-enactors in the reconstructed sod houses (Kathy, Dawn Taylor, Mike, Cole) – you really make L'Anse aux Meadows come alive. Dale Kennedy, thanks for introducing me to Bird Cove with its fascinating, complex archaeological history and for voyages of exploration to Quirpon island and elsewhere. (Bird Cove is one of the most important sites currently under excavation in Newfoundland/Labrador. It will be better known in the near future). Kevin Hartley and Jeff Browning for logistical support at Bird Cove; Wally Young and all his staff at the Plum Point Motel for generous support of the archaeological dig, and for hospitality at the conferences; Selma Barkham for stimulating conversation, for masses of information on the Basque presence in Bird Cove area and on the Labrador shore; for organizing those excellent conferences; and for contacts in the strangest of circles. Latonia, Tim, Micki, and all the crew (locals and imports) of the Bird Cove dig and the archaeological lab.

Gwen and Steve Knudsen of the Dark Tickle store, St. Lunaire-Griquet, are pioneers in making and marketing jams, sauces, jellies, pickles, spreads (and who knows what new this year) made from the wild berries of Newfoundland and Labrador. This should be a major spark for the kinds of small-scale industry this unique environment offers in abundance. When will you start marketing sweet gale, wild juniper berries, and cow parsnip seeds? Marie MacDonald and Kelly at Northern Delight, Gunner's Cove, and Kelly for guiding. Three cheers for the hot Newfie iceberg! Barb Genge of the Tuckamore Lodge merits special mention: you have been a major force in the regional business associations, and a voice of sanity, reason, and moderation in all discussion of the economic future of this wonderful land – and I won't forget your generosity. Justin – thanks for great guiding! Next time I will get those bear pictures! Colin Davis, park ranger at Pistolet Bay Provincial Park: I'm planning always to be that rookie whose photos you admired.

In St. Anthony there are the Hillyards (Jez and Gill), Bill Fitzgerald and Trudy O'Keefe for most generous hospitality and encouragement; Randy Letto and the Viking Trail Tourism Association; Kathy Letto and the staff at Norstead, the re-enactment Viking trading post at L'Anse aux Meadows; Bob Parsons for medicinal plant lore. Paul Alcock, Lewis, and Jack – thanks for moose, caribou, partridge, and the limestone barrens; for icebergs, whales, sea caves and seabirds. Thanks for the introduction to moose hunting – I got excellent photos! In Roddickton there are Dan and Karen Cox – Katie and Hannah sure liven up the place! Nova Scotia is the richer for your emigration. Gerty, Gerry, Paul, and the other Bromleys of Conche; Betty and Winse, thanks for countless kindnesses; Violet and Don; Joan and Rex; Mohan and Thama. The list could go on for pages.

I thank the whole town of Raleigh who have so actively taken on guardianship of the Burnt Cape, and to Sue Meades for leading the way. Vi and Ross Taylor, thanks for bed, breakfasts, unscheduled lunches and dinners, and less-visible support.

I want to thank staff of Gros Morne Park: Chip Bird; Colleen Kennedy of the Association; Anne Marceau and Mike Burzynski and the many rangers who have helped me in so many ways; Jacqui at Java Jack's for the best coffee north of Corner Brook; the Neils of Norris Point for their unforgettable B&B.

I owe a special debt to the folks at NF Historic Sites and Newfoundland Provincial Parks: Sharon Porter-Trask; Carol Ann Monk; Carol Ann Carter; Catherine Dempsey; Glen Ryan. Thanks very much for encouragement in its many forms.

Thanks to Peter J. Scott for stalwart service in the trenches – and I'm looking forward to Volume II; to Pierre Bertrand for scannings and other photographic help; and to Marie-Hélène Boyer for nursing this through its final stages.

Jolene – thanks for giving me the Newfoundland impetus, for 'seeing' the book before I did, and for all the encouragements.

Martin F. Kilmer
Ottawa, May 2002

Introduction

When the Norse adventurers reached the northern tip of Newfoundland's Great Northern Peninsula some time not too far off AD 1000, they found a landscape very much like what the modern traveler finds at L'Anse aux Meadows. There is an area of coastal plain, largely bog, with strips of permafrost (a land feature which geographers and geologists call a palsa bog) and numerous small ponds. Trees grow only near sea level; and there, short tangled trees – mostly spruce – grow close together to form virtually impenetrable thickets of the sort Newfoundlanders call 'tuckamore'. These trees, though rarely as much as a metre high, may be hundreds of years old. The upper slopes of the hills are treeless, with much bare rock and large areas of low ground cover - mosses, lichens, and low-growing plants such as crowberry, the three bearberries, bakeapple, and partridgeberry.

In the bogs there are dwarf birches, sweet gale, and a few other woody plants (larch, locally known as 'juniper', tends to grow the largest of these, usually on the outer edge; and black spruce can grow to a respectable size), but most of the vegetation is herbaceous, with many different mosses and lichens filling in where roots cannot yet take hold. There was more forest inland then. We know this from studying the ancient pollens, collected both from lake bottoms and from the sods used to build the houses on the archaeological site. European settlers have, over the past few centuries, cut most of the deciduous forest for lumber. The conifers are rapidly disappearing for use as firewood and – much more damaging to this fragile landscape than the small-scale uses of the local people – for pulpwood. A thousand years ago there may have been some trees on the Northern Peninsula tall enough to use for lumber for boat repair, even the occasional tree inland tall enough to make spars or even masts; but trees for shipbuilding (mostly repairs, as far as we can judge) were probably harvested in Labrador.

At Great Harbour Deep, the hills seem to overwhelm the small houses, fishing stages and stores along the water's edge.

The Norse had no reason to be concerned for preservation of their habitat. They could not know how much damage their land clearing was already causing in Iceland; they could not know the damage overgrazing would soon cause in Iceland and in Greenland. They could not know that trees they used for lumber or for fuel would not be replaced for hundreds of years.

We know, now, that the tuckamore is very ancient. We know that without protection, these trees have little chance of taking root, and less of growing to maturity in this climate which, though warmer now than it has been at any time in the past five hundred years, is still cold and windy. It is still cold enough, in fact, that spruces have to reproduce by cloning - the growing season is too short for their seed to mature. The near-constant wind also ensures that any growing tip that exposes itself above the mass will be dehydrated and killed over winter.

We also know that even the trees in the interior – slightly warmer and considerably better protected against wind – grow very slowly indeed. The trees cut by our generation will not be replaced by trees of the same kinds and of similar stature for several hundred years. This does **not** allow for sustainable harvest of large amounts of pulpwood. And yet, this is a remarkably generous region. Of the many plants that grow in the coastal portions of the Northern Peninsula and in southern coastal Labrador, a surprising number are usable as human food (either the whole plant or parts of it); and those which are not food plants have many other human uses.

Astrid Blue-eye (*Dawn Taylor*) spins yarn with a drop-spindle (her carding tools are on the bench beside her) in a reconstructed sod house at L'Anse aux Meadows.

Thanks to Dawn Taylor and to the *Viking Trail Tourism Association* for permission to publish this photograph.

All of the food plants can be harvested without damaging them and without damaging their environment. Harvesting must be done carefully; and mechanization is not an option for most of these plants. The bog soil, or precarious shallow soil built up on rock, is damaged very easily. Careless use of all-terrain vehicles and even snowmobiles tears out soil which has taken thousands of years to develop, and which will be replaced only in thousands of years. Any changes we make in this environment act quickly. Return to the previous condition may never come about (at least, not within our grandchildren's lifetime). Overfishing has already changed the sea of this region so much that some 'fish stocks' are likely never to recover. Many people of this region realize that their land resources are just as fragile as the sea's.

Tourists are coming to the Great Northern Peninsula in larger numbers than ever before. They come to see the unique landscape – often, to see what their ancestors saw. Some want to try local foods prepared in traditional ways, using traditional ingredients. One of the things this book is about is to help make these things possible. We can only prepare the foods if we maintain the environment, the soil, and the soil conditions that plants and animals require. People will come to see the unique landscape only as long as the landscape is there to see. We can do this all **only** if we protect and maintain this extremely fragile ecosystem.

Martin F. Kilmer
Ottawa, May 2002

Astrid Blue-eye (*Dawn Taylor*) tending her soup kettle in a reconstructed sod house at l'Anse aux Meadows

Thanks to Dawn Taylor and to the *Viking Trail Tourism Association* for permission to publish this photograph.

ctaea

Actaea
Actaea rubra f. neglecta

The white variant (note the short, stiff fruit stems and the black dot on each berry) and the red-berried – its fruit is almost the same color as Squashberry, but the stiff, almost spherical berry cluster is very different – are both equally toxic. The plant, in our region, is rarely over a metre high.

Actaea grows well in open woods, but can also be found in bright sunny locations

 This plant is extremely poisonous.

In this photograph, we see Actaea's distinctive composite leaves as well as the mature berries of the white variant.

In our region, actaea is most commonly found at, or near, sea-level. It prefers more sheltered spots than this at l'Anse aux Meadows.

lnus

Mountain alder
Alnus crispa (Ait.) Pursh

The alder, which springs up so enthusiastically, produces an abundance of fine flexible twigs which can be put to many uses: they can be woven into baskets and fences, fed to livestock, and used for many purposes in the garden. Some aboriginal people stripped the inner bark for dyeing, producing a clear yellow. The outer bark produces red, brown, or black. These dyes may be used for wood, wool or skin. As a medicine, alder's silver-grey bark is traditionally employed as a febrifuge and an astringent and against ulcerations, though some people are allergic to its pollen. Its reddish colouring and its dyeing uses have led people in Siberia and in Northern Europe to use alder as a ritual substitute for red ochre.

Buds of male catkins.

Identification – Alders have dark green leaves that are rough in appearance and to the touch. They often have old fruit remaining on the branches which look like tiny pine cones. This species differs from the other on the island by having oval winter buds which are attached directly by the base. Also, the leaves have 7-8 pairs of main lateral veins.

Distribution – All across Canada and south in the mountains of the United States in New England and Wisconsin.

Speckled alder
Alnus rugosa (DuRoi) Spreng.

Alders have a number of medicinal uses. Leaves and bark have been used for intermittent fevers, inflammation of the tonsils, and swellings and sprains. Charcoal made from the wood was found to be light and the very best for gunpowder.

◄ Male catkins expanded.

Identification – This differs from Mountain Alder in having 10 or more pairs of veins in each leaf and the winter bud on a short stalk.

Distribution – Eastern Canada to Saskatchewan and the northern of the eastern United States (Wisconsin eastwards and south to Pennsylvania).

Ripe chuckley pear fruit at Great Harbour Deep.

Amelanchier

Chuckley pear
Amelanchier spp

Amelanchier spicata is *hägmistel* in Swedish. Chuckley pears are also called wild pears and Indian pears on the island (on the Northern Peninsula, often just "pears") and have many names elsewhere: juneberry, serviceberry, shadbush, and sarvis and one species is the Saskatoon of the Canadian Prairies.

Young fruit. ➤

Identification – There are six species on the island. They all have distinctive flowers and fruit but require careful attention to minute details to distinguish from one another. The winter buds are narrow and the scales have hairs on the margin. The leaves are thin and have fine toothing on the margins. Most on the Northern Peninsula are Bartram's chuckley pears (Amelanchier bartramiana) which has only 1-3 flowers (or fruit) in a cluster. It is also found in Labrador.

Distribution – This species is found in eastern North America from Ontario to Newfoundland and south to Georgia. It is found commonly across Newfoundland and in southern Labrador.

▲
Chuckley pear fertilized ovaries.

◄ Chuckley pear flowers.

These fruit (pictured to the right) were growing alongside a pond near Goulds. Apple rust (introduced accidentally by European settlers – it travelled with the apples) unfortunately is very happy to grow on these fruit – destroying the great majority before they can ripen. They grow rather well (not, unfortunately, in large numbers) in open woodland on the Northern Peninsula. I have photographed the flowers on the Fox Farm hill (July 1997) and have seen them along Philips Garden walk at Port au Choix and in the park at Hawkes Bay. The hill above the visitors' parking lot at the Roddickton 'hospital' has many bushes, heavily pruned by moose, but with a rich yield despite that.

The fruit are delicious right off the tree, and are superb eaten along with a good French vanilla ice cream.

Above: ripe fruit.
Inset: early stage.

ᚳHUᚳKLᛊY ᚷRUNᛏ

A variation on blueberry grunt. My thanks to my sister, Noelie Angevine, for the variations (MK)

1/2 tsp vanilla
1 qt chuckley pears
1/2 c water with 3 tbsp lemon juice
1/2 c sugar (3/4 c brown sugar, packed)
1 1/2 c flour
2 tsp baking powder

1/4 tsp salt
1 tsp sugar
2 tbsp butter or margarine
milk
1/4 c Drambuie
(*or fruit juice if preferred*)

Heat chuckley pears, water and sugar slowly until fruit begins to soften; bring to boil. Simmer gently for 20 mins (Don't let it scorch!) while making dumplings. Mix together flour, baking powder, salt and sugar. Cut in butter and add enough milk to make a soft dough. Drop dumpling dough by tablespoonsful onto hot berries. Makes about ten dumplings. Cover tightly and cook 15 minutes without raising lid. Dumplings will double in size. Serve hot, spooning sauce over dumplings. Top with cream or ice cream.

Andromeda

Bog-rosemary
Andromeda glaucophylla Link

Aboriginal people used the leaves to make tea (steep, never boil or simmer). Shepherds in Europe and North America had to be careful as the leaves are quite toxic to sheep and other livestock.

Bog rosemary fruit in August. ➤

Identification – This evergreen shrub of the bogs has leaves which look like those of the culinary herb, rosemary. The flowers are exquisite translucent shell pink urns which are narrowed at their opening and hang down in clusters. The mature fruit are dry brown capsules, in their immature phase an attractive pink. The narrow quilted leaves with whitened veins distinguish this species.

Distribution – Found from Greenland through eastern North America to Pennsylvania and west to Wisconsin.

! *Not recommended for eating*

▲
Andromeda flowers at Micky's Hill.
Inset: Flowers.

▲ Detail of both flower types of Angelica

Angelica

Close-up: flowers of Angelica.

Botanists are not in agreement over the presence of this plant in Newfoundland in Viking times. There are both a European and a native variety.

Its purple stems make Angelica easier to distinguish from its cousins Alexander's, Scotch lovage, and Heracleum maximum (cow parsnip).

 Do not harvest the plant in the wild if you do not know how to distinguish it from (poisonous) water hemlock. (Guédon)

Identification – This is a big, sturdy plant with leaves that look like huge celery leaves and the umbels of flowers have small balls of white flowers.

Distribution – A species from Europe and western Asia which also grows in Greenland, Labrador and adjacent parts of Quebec.

This plant, which was widely cultivated in Europe, was used in cooking, baking, confectionery and liqueurs, and as a medicine. The root helped with stomach and bowel upsets, and a tea made from the roots was used for nervous headaches. The candied stems are transformed into a delicacy in Europe and especially in France, while the leaves and roots are believed to have relaxing and anti-inflammatory properties. The fresh roots, like the rest of the plant, are poisonous; they become edible when dried or cooked. Tea can be made with the dried leaves. As a smudge, angelica is used in conjunction with sweat baths or used by itself in a ritual setting.

! *Always cook before eating.*

Alexanders
Angelica atropurpurea L.

The roots were highly prized by aboriginal people who used it medicinally and as a talisman. It was found in every home and was frequently carried by settlers for good luck in hunting and gambling. The fresh root was considered poisonous but the dried root was used as food. Leaves and stems were eaten in various ways. Both uses and properties are similar to those of angelica (see previous entry). Alexanders is an important native medicine. It is called "hunting root" by some of the Algonquin native people who say it attracts deer. Its dried roots used to be smoked by several groups including Missouri tribes (see Erichsen-Brown, 1979:247) to alleviate colds and respiratory ailments. It is one of the sacred plants used in the sweat lodge.

Flower buds: Alexanders.

Identification – This is a big plant, in sheltered locations, with leaves that look like those of ash or elder. The umbels of white flowers have smaller umbels like dill. The stems are smooth and purple-stained.

Distribution – This species is found from southern Labrador to Wisconsin and south to Virginia.

Flowers of Alexanders.

 Do not harvest the plant in the wild if you do not know how to distinguish it from (poisonous) water hemlock. (Guédon)

Its smoke is soft and sweet with a penetrating licorice or anise-like flavor, becoming stronger than it first seems, especially when seeds are used.

Use the dry seeds, or the powdered bark or the dried roots of cultivated plants. The fresh leaves or a concoction made with any part of the plant may be placed on the hot stones of the sauna. (Guédon)

! *Always cook before eating.*

Umbelliferae

The flowers of the Umbelliferae are typically bisexual. In this family, however, a common ploy is used to make the flowers more noticeable to pollinators. They are grouped and then the outer flowers are modified to make a 'border'. We use similar devices in crocheted doilies. As far as I know all of the flowers are bisexual irrespective of their petal modifications (PS).

◄ A roadside ditch (this one beside the road to Fishing Point) provides excellent habitat for any of the local Umbellifers.

Arctostaphylos

Flowers of Alpine bearberry (greenish).

When the aboriginal people passed the pipe they were usually smoking leaves of this plant.

 It has an alkaloid in it which will produce a mild sedative effect but should not be used frequently as it can damage the liver. Smoking was only done during special cere-monies.

Identification – A trailing shrub with oval leaves which are broadest towards the tip and quilted. There is a fringe of hair along the margins at the base of the leaf and teeth all around the margin. The leaves turn red in the autumn. The flowers are white and urn-shaped and borne in clusters at the tips of branches. The berries are black when ripe and persist over winter. They are rather bitter, especially the seeds. I have not found a cooking method that improves this, but plan to try cooking them with acid fruit (par-tridgeberry; lemon juice).

Distribution – This species is found throughout Newfoundland and Labrador. It is a circumpolar species that extends south into most of the Canadian provinces but not the Maritimes.

Alpine bearberry, early August. By ➤
September, these berries will be black.

Micky's Hill, upper slopes; much of the darker green is Alpine bearberry.

Fruit of Alpine bearberry in July.

Red bearberry
Arctostaphylos rubra (Rehder & Wilson) Fern.

The leaves of this and the other bearberries were dried and ground with tobacco or red willow and used as a smoking mixture. A tea made with the stems, leaves, and berries was used by many tribes of aboriginal people for a sprained or aching back.

Ripe red bearberry, Burnt Cape.

Identification – Similar in growth habit to alpine bearberry but the leaves have a smoother surface and there is no fringe of hair at the base. The fruit are scarlet, juicy, sweeter and better tasting than the Alpine bearberry. They do not persist over winter.

Distribution – Found in much the same range as alpine bearberry but more southern and absent from Greenland and Europe.

The bare limestone of the Burnt Cape hosts few plants. The red bearberry by the pink cairn is a rarity. Across the harbour is the little town of Raleigh.

Bearberry, evergreen bearberry (Swedish mjölon)
Arctostaphylos uva-ursi (L.) Spreng.

The leaves and stems of this plant were used in Sweden and Russia for tanning leather. The leaves have been used through the centuries for kidney and bladder complaints and the berries were cooked with meat to season the broth. This is a sacred and powerful plant, used in healing and other ceremonies. Its berries are considered both medicine and food. In Europe, bearberry leaves are used to make an astringent and diuretic tea. In North America, this bearberry's leaf is smoked either alone or in combination with tobacco or red willow by many of the Aboriginal people; it is one ingredient of Kinnikinnik mix. The Great Lakes Indian people brought it to the medicine lodge for ritual smudging. It is considered by some to enhance psychic powers.

Ripe bearberry, Burnt Cape (Microhabitat).

Sturtevant speaks of dried leaves mixed with tobacco by Crees and Chinook and Inuit north of Churchill. "Its dry, farinaceous berry is utterly inedible." Sturtevant did not try cooking it.

Identification – A sprawling evergreen shrub that can form quite a large mat. The leaves are broader towards the tip and the surface is more matte than glossy. It has no teeth around the margin. The flowers are urn-shaped and white or pale pink. The fruit are scarlet and pulpy but not tasty.

Distribution – A circumboreal species found across North America, Europe, and Asia. It is found in Greenland and Iceland. The Burnt Cape has this in abundance. This is the bearberry most commonly found on the Northern Peninsula.

For smudging, use the dried and powdered leaves or dried roots. (Guédon)

They are unpleasant if eaten raw; they have little flavour, and chewing turns them into a flour-like substance. Thirty seconds' frying transforms them: they become an excellent addition to salads, and, according to Peterson, are quite nice with sugar and cream.

The leaves make a pleasant tea.

◄ Ripe berries, Burnt Cape.

Aronia

Purple chokeberry
Aronia prunifolia (Marsh.) Rehder

While the berries were used by tribes in the northeastern United States to make pemmican, most agree that the berries are too astringent for eating. They have been used for colds and digestive upsets.

Flowers.➤

Identification – This short shrub of peatlands has a general hairiness about it. The leaves are oval and broader towards the tip with teeth around the margin. The upper surface is a dark glossy green and the under surface has a felt of white hairs. The flowers are white or pinkish and look like typical flowers of the rose family. The common name, chokeberry, describes what it is like to eat them. The fruit are glossy black and slightly fuzzy.

Peterson (1977, p.220) says the chokeberry can be used like blueberry, and that it makes excellent jellies and jams. The purple chokeberry is not abundant; it also may not be as sweet as its more southerly siblings, the black and the red chokeberries.

Distribution – This is a plant of eastern North America which reaches its northern limit in Newfoundland.

This is abundant on the lower slope of Signal Hill at St. John's, overlooking the Narrows, and along roadsides and beside ponds on the Avalon. It is less common farther north.

➤
◄ Buds and flowers.

triplex

Smooth orache is an excellent potherb that is found in quantity along many of the beaches. It can vary considerably in height depending upon what nutrients are available to it; a dead fish is most welcome. It was often used by fishers when they would set up camps in northern harbours. It also adds a pleasant accent in salads.

Flower spikes of smooth orache are pale pink at the tip.

Smooth orache is a cousin of lambsquarter, a common edible 'weed' in much of the northern hemisphere. Smooth orache is the aristocrat, lambsquarter something of a plebeian.

Identification – As a member of the goosefoot family it has leaves which somewhat resemble the feet of geese; broadened towards the tip and with three lobes. The lumpy flower spikes have leaves along their length and are relatively compact. The rounded clusters of green flowers are not particularly noticeable but the leaves are distinctive. They resemble arrowheads with sharp scallops around the margins.It grows on coastal beaches and in salt marshes.

Distribution – Smooth Orache is found around the north Atlantic - northwest Europe, Iceland, and Greenland into Hudson Bay in North America and south to southern New England.

The flowers of leatherleaf are an excellent example of what botanists call urn-shaped flowers.

Chamaedaphne

Leatherleaf
Chamædaphne calyculata (L.) Moench

The leaves can be steeped (never boiled or simmered) to make a tea and aboriginal people used the tea for fevers and the leaves as a poultice for inflammation. The dainty flowers are reminiscent of lilies-of-the-valley.

Flowers. ➤

Identification – A short evergreen shrub of the peatlands which has dull green leaves with brownish scales on their surfaces. The leaves are oval with a rounded tip and tend to come off the stem and point upwards. The flowers are lovely white urns which hang in a row from a gracefully-arching stem. The fruit are dry brown capsules.

Distribution – This is a circumboreal species. In North America, it is found across boreal Canada and down the Appalachians.

Flowers - detail.

These Clintonia bloom in the shade of alder and fir at Burnt Cape.
Growing with them are Labrador tea and both varieties of bunchberry.

Empetrum

Purple crowberry
Empetrum atropurpureum Fern. & Wieg.

This species has a restricted distribution and it is not immediately obvious to most that it is different from the commoner crowberry. One's stomach would probably not notice a difference either. Uses are the same as for crowberry.

▲ Male flowers of *Empetrum spp.* (probably simple 'blackberry') bloom on 19 May at L'Anse aux Meadows. It was snowing. The female flowers, from which the berries develop, are on separate plants nearby.

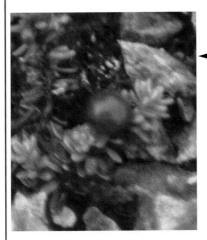

◄ Single berry of pink crowberry graces a Burnt Cape plant - the whole plant less than three cm.

Identification – Purple crowberry is difficult to distinguish for a casual observer. The twigs are densely covered with white hairs and the fruit are dark red to purple with a whitish bloom.

Distribution – Purple crowberry has a scattered distribution in northeastern North America from Newfoundland and Labrador to Lake Superior and south into northern New England.

These puddings also work well with blueberries, or with a mix of blueberries and crowberries, reducing sugar to taste.

CROWBERRY PUDDING

1 egg or 3 tbsp oil
2/3 c molasses
3 tbsp melted shortening
1 tsp vanilla
1 3/4 c flour
1 tsp baking powder
1/2 tsp baking soda

1/2 tsp salt
1 tsp cinnamon
1/2 tsp mace
1/4 tsp ginger *(or 1 tsp fresh grated fine)*
1/2 c cold water
1 c crowberries

Beat egg and stir in the molasses, melted shortening and vanilla. Sift dry ingredients together (or stir with a fork) and add, alternating small amounts of the water. Fold in blackberries. Put in a pudding bag and boil three hours; or pour into 8-inch mold and steam three hours.

Pink crowberry
Empetrum eamesii Fern. & Wieg.

Male crowberry flowers, mid-May.

In the Red Bay region of Labrador, this berry is called 'wine berry' or 'sand berry' – 'sand berry' because it grows at the margins of sandy beaches and in shallow sandy soil. Dr. William Shippard, who grew up in the Baie Verte region of north-central Newfoundland, tells me that these were called 'soldier berries' – named after the 'Red Coats' of English soldiers? These beauties, called 'pink blackberry' in Newfoundland, are found at higher elevations and would look lovely in a fruit salad. The colour is interesting to note as it can vary from a pale translucent pink to quite a rosy hue.

Identification – The fruit which look like pink pearls distinguish this species.

Distribution – It is found around the Gulf of St. Lawrence - Cape Breton Island, southeastern Labrador, and in a number of localities across the island of Newfoundland. Much less common than the black-fruited variety.

Ripe crowberries with immature partridgeberries.

STEAMED CROWBERRY PUDDING

1 1/2 c. flour
1/4 tsp salt
1/2 c. sugar
2 tsp baking powder

1 1/4 c. crowberries
1/4 c. margarine
1/2 c. milk
1 beaten egg or 3 tbsp oil

Mix dry ingredients in a bowl. Add berries, milk (it works best with the addition of warm milk), and egg or oil, stirring lightly to make a batter. Pour into greased 1 quart mold. Place over boiling water and steam 1 hr. Serve hot with sauce:

1/2 c. brown sugar
1 tbsp cornstarch
1 tsp butter or margarine

1 c. hot water
pinch salt
1 tsp vanilla

Mix sugar, salt, and cornstarch in saucepan; add hot water (slowly at first to avoid lumps) and boil until thickened. Then add butter and vanilla.

Ripe pink crowberries.

Crowberry, blackberry(Swedish vanligt kråkbär)
Empetrum nigrum L.

A local name for this plant is blackberry heath which notes its berry and the plant's overall appearance. The fruit are easy to pick and are usually found on headlands where it is so nice to recline on a sparkling autumn day. The berries are usually baked in a cottage pudding and included in an accompanying molasses sauce.

Slightly bitter raw. Cook with lemon juice, serve with cream and sugar. Jamie Pye at Red Bay tells me that 'blackberry bawn' - the turf and 'blackberries' complete - used to be thrown into the smoker for smoking salmon. His father and grandfather both used this by preference, living in Lodge Bay (and Caroll's Cove in the summer). The smoker was made from a fifty-gallon drum to the top of which was attached a string of sections of stove pipe (to concentrate the smoke); the salmon was hung inside the stove pipe.

▲
Green crowberry in late July

Makes a good jam: add lemon juice; mix half-and-half with partridgeberry, cranberry, or another acid fruit. Cook with apple or add pectin.

Identification - Crowberries are mat-forming evergreen shrubs which look something like diminutive spruce boughs. The flowers are very small and open in the earliest days of spring. The berry is spherical but slightly flattened on the ends and has a dimple. It is matte black and juicy. It is found in abundance on headlands and is a great favourite of migrating birds.

Distribution - This is a circumpolar and circumboreal species which ranges south in the mountains to California and New England. It is found in Greenland and Iceland as well as northern Europe and Asia.

STEAMED BLACKBERRY PUDDING

1 1/2 c flour
1/4 tsp salt
1/2 c sugar
2 tsp baking powder

1 1/4 c blackberries
1/4 c margarine
1/2 c milk
1 beaten egg or 3 tbsp oil

Mix dry ingredients in a bowl. Add berries, milk, and egg or oil, stirring lightly to make a batter. Pour into greased 1 quart mold. Place over boiling water and steam 1 hr.

Serve hot with sauce:
1/2 c brown sugar
1 tbsp cornstarch
1 tsp butter or margarine

1 c hot water
pinch salt
1 tsp vanilla

Mix sugar, salt, and cornstarch in saucepan; add hot water (slowly at first to avoid lumps) and boil until thickened. Then add butter and vanilla.

The replica sod houses at l'Anse aux Meadows in a late May snowstorm.

BLACK AND BLUEBERRY APPLE PIE

2 c. peeled chopped apples
1 c. crowberries
1 c. blueberries
1/2 c. sugar (or 3/4 c. brown sugar)

1/2 tsp nutmeg
dash salt
1 tbsp lemon or lime juice
1 tbsp flour

For the pie pastry, follow any pastry recipe you like. Lattice or vented whole crust both work fine.

Line pie plate with pastry. Combine remaining ingredients and mix well. Turn into prepared pie shell. Cover with remaining pastry (vented top crust or lattice). For a nicer brown on top crust, brush lightly with egg white or with sugar water. Bake at 375F for 45 minutes.

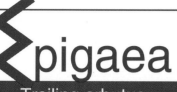

Epigaea

Trailing arbutus
Epigaea repens L.

Trailing arbutus is found largely in open woodland and in clearings. Its leaves are oval and leathery, its trailing woody stems brown and hairy. Its flowers are white to pink, growing in clusters.

The corolla (flower tube) is tasty on its own or as an addition to salads. This fragrant flower of the spring can be eaten as a nibble while hiking through the woods. They taste spicy and a bit acidic.

In many jurisdictions, trailing arbutus is protected. Check before picking.

Trailing arbutus flowers in Gros Morne Park. ➤

Identification –The trailing arbutus is a prostrate evergreen shrub which forms small patches in the forest. The leaves are leathery and shiny and there are reddish-brown hairs on many parts of the plant.

Distribution – It has a limited distribution in southwestern Newfoundland where it mainly grows on forest floors. It occurs from southern Manitoba to western Newfoundland and south to Florida.

Flowers, early August, near Bay Bulls.

Epilobium

Fireweed
Epilobium angustifolium L.

This plant covers burnt-over areas and, when in bloom, makes them look ablaze again. The young shoots have been used by many peoples as a potherb.

The 'stands' of this are easily spotted in late summer and early fall when it is in bloom. Go back in early spring and cut the young plants: cook and eat like asparagus.

Often the first plant to grow in burnt-over areas (hence its name) and in other disturbed places. Common along the roadside of the Viking Trail itself, with particularly abundant stands just north of Gros Morne Park.

The flowers at the tip are the last to open.

Fireweed flowers.

Identification – Many aspects of this plant are long and elegant. The stem is tall, the leaves are long and narrow, and the seed capsules are like short knitting needles. The capsules release fluffy seeds over a period of time as they slowly split open.

Distribution – Fireweed is a circumboreal species that extends to California in the west and North Carolina in the east.

Fragaria

▲
Ripe strawberries.

Strawberries are always a special treat in the summer but they were dried by the native Americans for winter use to maintain health. The fruit have been used medicinally for urinary tract problems and the leaves and roots are well known as an astringent to treat bowel complaints.

Identification –Wood strawberry has the 'seeds' (which are, in fact, the fruit) stuck on the surface of the fleshy part of the 'fruit' while in the common strawberry they are set in pits. The terminal tooth of the leaflets is about the same length as the adjacent ones in the wood strawberry and it is shorter in the common strawberry. The flowers are a little wider in the common strawberry (each petal about 7-10 mm long in the common strawberry and 5-7 mm in the wood strawberry).

Distribution – The wood strawberry occurs in northeastern North America and in Europe.

Flowers (one only half open) and ➤
buds of *Fragaria sp.*

Common strawberry
Fragaria virginiana Duchesne

Identification – *In the common strawberry the 'seeds' are set in pits in the surface of the flesh. In the common strawberry the terminal tooth of the leaflets is shorter than the adjacent teeth. The flowers of the common strawberry are a little wider (each petal about 7-10 mm long in the common strawberry and 5-7 mm in the wood strawberry).*

Distribution – *The common strawberry grows from Newfoundland to Alberta and south to Oklahoma in the west, and Georgia in the east.*

⋏
Strawberry leaves showing typical three leaflets. As is common, this example of *Fragaria virginiana* is in a field; *F. vesca* prefers open woods.

⋏
Without a clear image of the whole leaf, even a detailed photograph of the flower cannot identify the species.

▲ *Gaultheria hispidula* (snowberry) fruit at Bird Cove in August.

Gaultheria

Creeping snowberry
Gaultheria hispidula (L.) Bigel

There are several common names for this on the island: capillaire, maidenhair berry, magna-tea berry, Indian tea berry, and variations of these. On Fogo island, they are called Dominion berries. The Chippewa and others used the leaves for tea and the tea was also used, therapeutically, for asthma. The fresh leaves are still used by Aboriginal people and European immigrants as an aromatic and strengthening tea (six 6-inch sprigs make a pleasant cup), or chewed to make teeth clean and breath fresh. The berries may be crushed and applied to fresh wounds to promote clotting and healing. For toothache, a snowberry should be bruised and held to the tooth - it reduces pain and can induce numbness.

At Burnt Cape, these snowberries grow in a deep cutting in the limestone.

Identification – A delicate spreading evergreen plant which has short rusty-brown bristles all over it, including the fruit. The leaves are small and taper evenly to each end. The flowers are tiny and fragile, and the fruit is actually a dry capsule which is encapsulated by the sepals which become fleshy. The white 'fruit' has a delicate wintergreen flavour.

Distribution – A boreal plant which occurs from British Columbia to southern Labrador and Newfoundland and then south to North Carolina.

These grow in sheltered spots in woods (they seem particularly happy under spruce; leaves and fruit are often concealed in mosses) in many places on the Northern Peninsula. I have seen them at L'Anse aux Meadows; on Fox Farm hill at St Anthony; in woods near the archaeological dig site on the Dog Peninsula (Bird Cove/Plum Point); along the forest roads around Roddickton; in sheltered, well-watered cuttings in the limestone of the Burnt Cape. For smudging, use the dried shredded leaves. (Guédon)

People possessed of very great patience may collect enough teaberries to make a very nice jam (MK).

Geum

Purple avens, water avens
Geum rivale L.

This species is sometimes called chocolate root as the root (rhizome) can be boiled and sweetened to make a chocolate-tasting drink. It works best if brewed in warm milk.

Flower and buds of water ➤ avens.

◄ *Geum rivale* at Pistolet Bay Provincial Park.

Identification – *The leaves are hairy and have a number of lobes at their tips. The flowers are nodding with yellow petals suffused with purple. The fruit follow in heads of plumed 'seeds'. It grows in wet places like wet meadows.*

Distribution –*Water avens occurs right across Canada, south to New Mexico in the west and New Jersey in the east. It is also found in Iceland, Europe, and western Asia.*

Typical habitat of water avens in the margin of wet woodland near a pond.

◄ Skeletal cow parsnip overlooking the Gulf of St. Laurence/Strait of Belle Isle near Daniel's Harbour. The seed head has lost its seeds over winter, and we see the fledgling new leaves around the base of the stalk.

The cow parsnip delights in disturbed ground, so much so that archaeologists use it as an index of human activity: Where it grows most enthusiastically, humans have been active. It is particularly common in recently-abandoned garden plots. It likes fertile, well-watered soil.

Justin Pittman of Sop's Arm tells me that his father and uncle used the leaf of cow parsnip for headache relief. Place the leaf in a cloth and bruise it gently. Apply the poultice to the part of the head that hurts. (MK)

Insectivores

Round-leafed sundew
Drosera rotundifolia L.

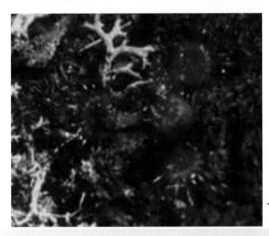

This wonderful little plant is often noticed while berry-picking on the bogs when you try to locate the buzzing - caused by a fly trying to escape from the sticky leaves. There have been a few medicinal uses suggested but the most encouraging report is that "in America it has been advocated as a cure for old age" (Grieve, 1930 in Erichsen-Brown).

◄ Round-leafed sundew on bog soil

Identification – The small rosette of rounded leaves beset with hairs tipped by glistening glands is distinctive. The flower stalk rises like a plume of smoke and has tiny white flowers.

Distribution – This species occurs from Greenland to Alaska and south to California in the west and northern Florida in the east. It also occurs in Eurasia.

An insect-eating plant. The enzymes on the tiny round leaves work to digest insects to make up for the poor nutrition of the bog soil in which it grows.

43

Pitcher plant
Saracenia purpurea

Newfoundland's provincial flower's leaves grow as vertical tubes in which water collects – along with any insects unfortunate enough to investigate them. Their nutrients are gradually absorbed.

The nodding purple flower of the pitcher plant, with its hard-looking green center, stands above most marsh plants in the places where it grows

▼

Identification – This carnivorous plant is the provincial flower for the province of Newfoundland and Labrador. It was suggested by Queen Victoria. Its champagne-flute-like leaves are partially filled with water and the insects captured there provide supplementary nutrients as the bogs where they grow are nutrient-poor. Also called huntsman's cup, it provides the same for woodsmen who drink the water. Some small animals live in the leaves. The flowers are tall and bold. The deep liver-purple petals drop after a short time but the stiff sepals remain.

Distribution – The pitcher plant grows on peatlands through much of eastern North America and across northern Canada to Alaska.

Pitcher plant in an upland bog along Green Gardens trail in Gros Morne Park in early July.

While wandering on peatlands you may think that you have found a violet in mid-summer but it is probably a Butterwort. The single violet-like flower atop a stalk arises from the broad, yellow-green leaves. These leaves have sticky hairs, are rolled up slightly around the margins, and appear shiny, as if smeared with butter, hence its common name. It is a carnivore and will digest any insects that stick to the leaves.

◄ Butterwort leaves

Identification – The single violet-like flower and the rosette of distinctive leaves make this plant easy to identify.

Distribution – Butterwort grows from Greenland to Alaska; south to Washington and Minnesota in the western United States and south to northern New England in the east.

Butterwort blooms here in company with blueberry and others.

▲
The flower of butterwort is a lovely pale purple, with a tinge of white. It stands about ten cm. above the rosette of leaves, making it difficult to get the whole plant in focus. Pinguicula is high-ly variable in size: I have seen individuals with leaves 6-10 cm long; and (on the Burnt Cape, for example) some which a quarter would cover completely.

Iris is the showiest of the flowers blooming near the reconstructed sod houses at L'Anse aux Meadows.

Iris

Iris, blue flag, blue flag iris
Iris versicolor L.

The lovely flowers open in late June (July in the north) and decorate many a wet site on the island. Common on exposed headlands, along the edges of bogs, along roadsides. Usually shorter than domesticated varieties, and much more hardy. There is a particularly lovely strain at L'Anse aux Meadows, growing in large numbers near the reconstructed sod houses.

! *Unpleasant side effects make it undesireable as smudge*

◄ Iris in full bloom at Fishing Point, St. Anthony, late July 1997. In 2001, iris bloomed at Fishing Point in late June; and many had two flowers, rather than the singles universal in 1997.

Identification – The broad leaves which clasp each other to make a spreading fan arise from plump rhizomes. The fat seed capsules have three tiers of flat, brown, pie-shaped seeds. Another species, beach-head flag (I. setosa Pall.), is found on headlands and beaches around the coast. It differs in subtle shapes of parts in the flower.

Distribution – This species is found in eastern North America from Labrador to Manitoba and south to Pennsylvania.

This violet-blue flower is better known for its roots or rhizomes which were widely, though often erroneously, employed against all sorts of health problems. The plant is poisonous with all kinds of side effects including headache and gastro-intestinal problems and must be used with a great deal of caution. With the mashed roots, native healers made poultices for wounds and abscesses or a concoction or wash for sores; while the people of the lower Mississipi regions included taking iris root decoctions as part of their communal purgative rituals. (Guédon)

! *Not recommended for eating.*

An iris bud begins to unfurl. The white flower behind is an arctic chickweed.

49

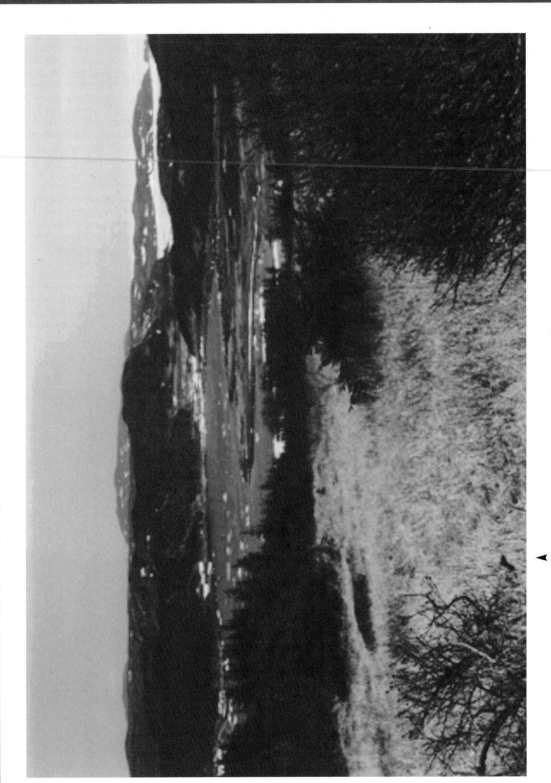

Juniper grows well along the edges of clearings like this one on Micky's Hill, Griquet-St. Lunaire.

Juniperus

Common juniper (Swedish *en*)
Juniperus communis L.

An Icelandic manuscript from 1475 notes that juniper is called fire tree in Greek because a fire covered with its ashes will stay alive for almost a whole year. There is also a long list of ailments for which this plant was used: diarrhoea, disease of the small intestine, loosening and expelling the afterbirth, mental troubles, epilepsy, and toothache.

Locally called 'spruce', as the name 'juniper' is already applied to the tree known elsewhere as tamarack, larch (etc.). In the area around Quirpon (and probably elsewhere on the Island) a tea made from the fruit of the juniper has long been used to treat urinary tract complaints. It is apparently diuretic: I (MK) was recently told of a man whose late-stage abdominal cancer had 'shut off his water'. This tea caused remarkable improvement. A tea made with the fruit used to be given to ewes shortly after lambing, though my sources could not tell me what effect it was thought to produce. *The Dictionary of Newfoundland English* (Toronto 1982/1990:282) under 'juniper tea' - made with the berries - cites an informant (M 70-15, whose name has escaped the index): 'I afterwards learned that the juniper had some special medicinal qualities found to be very beneficial to the mother after childbirth'. *The Dictionary of Newfoundland English* (Toronto 1982/1990:426) under 'saffron' - defined as *Juniperus communis* - gives the following: "Saffron is not very common. The old people used to use it for young girls who got pregnant before they were married. They used to steep the roots and have the girls drink the tea." The *Dictionary* does not explain what resulted from this use but we strongly disrecommend it.

The berries of juniper take three years to➤ mature fully. The blue berries here are in their second summer.

Identification – A sprawling coniferous shrub which seems spiny because of the sharp-tipped needles. The dark green needles have their margins rolled under and there is a white stripe down the middle of the upper surface and the lower surface is whitened. The 'berries' are blue-black with a white bloom and are the flavouring of gin.

Distribution – This species is widespread in North America, Greenland, Europe, and Asia. Found often intermingled with sweet gale, blueberry, and/or partridgeberry.

The berries in their younger state (pale green to blue-green) are a fine trail snack, and are surprisingly good mixed with sweeter fruit such as blueberry in baking (in the proportion one juniper to ten blueberry).

The mature third-year berries (dark blue to black, drier and more brittle than the young berries) are delicious added to stews (a dozen or so added to a stew meant for six or eight people). They may be crushed in a mortar and sprinkled over meats or fish before cooking. They are particularly pleasant if used in combination with leaves or fruit of sweet gale (*qv*).

The common Juniper is found both in North America and in Europe as well as in Northern Asia and Siberia. Though slightly toxic, it is a well-recognized antiseptic, a good agent against infections, and a diuretic. It has anti-inflammatory properties and it stimulates uterine contractions. It may cause hallucinations. The common juniper produces the "seeds" used to flavor gin. It is used as a spice in Northern European cooking.

The needles are used by many North American Aboriginal people as an antiseptic. A medicinal tea against arthritis pain, scurvy, colds and flu is made with its needles and its berries; poultices of needles and/or berries are made to combat infections and protect open wounds. Juniper branches were laid on the stones of the sweat lodge.

Try dried and crushed berries or crushed roots or green tips of branches, or fresh or dried needles for smudging. Use fresh needles or branches to steam over slow fires. Use the roots of the common juniper for denser smoke and for shamanic rituals. (Guédon)

 Do not use as smudge when children or pregnant women are present.

◄ This heavily-laden specimen I found on the Burnt Cape; on Quirpon Island (November 1998) I found many plants this rich or richer.

What look here like pale green berries are in fact the tiny flowers from which the berries will form. The first-year berries are very much this colour.

Trailing juniper
Juniperus horizontalis Moench

This shrub hugs the ground on headlands and weaves among the other plants there. There is often a variation in the colour of the plant in each site, ranging from dark green to a bluish white.

 Do not use as smudge when children or pregnant women are present.

Identification – The stems are tightly clothed in scale-like needles and the fruit are three-parted resinous berries. A related species, common juniper (Juniperus communis L.), is more upright and spreading and has sharp needles which stand off from the stems.

Distribution – This is a northern species that grows from Newfoundland to Alaska and south to Nebraska in the west and New England in the east. Much less frequent in our region than the common juniper. I have not cooked with this, but find the raw berries much harsher than those of the common juniper.

This specimen grows near salt water on the Dog Peninsula, Bird Cove. Phillips Garden walk at Port au Choix, which overlooks the Gulf of St. Lawrence, has trailing juniper in abundance.

Kalmia

Sheep laurel, lambkill
Kalmia angustifolia L.

This is a species of drier sites that is a major problem in the forests of the island. The roots exude a substance that inhibits the growth of other plants, particularly conifers, and has caused considerable problems for reforestation after a fire or lumber harvesting. One local name of this plant (at L'Anse aux Meadows) is 'saffron'. The common name 'lambkill' may come from the fact that pregnant ewes which eat this plant are likely to abort or miscarry. In addition to this, lambs and older animals have a powerful craving for green matter in the spring and since this is green in the spring it is eaten with lethal results. This is also from Peter J. Scott's personal experience raising goats.

Fertilized ovaries of sheep laurel. Ripe fruit are brown and dry.

It used to be said that to avoid pregnancy, a girl should have some of this in her shoes. We do not guarantee this method as efficacious.

The flowers of lambkill grow on radiating horizontal stems; the year's new growth shows above the flowers. The leaves are generally flat, not rolled like those of bog laurel.

Identification – An extremely common shrub which has leaves in loose whorls of threes and pink saucerlike flowers which grow in a ring around the upper stem. The stamens, which are held in pockets of the flower, are released like a catapult when an insect disturbs them. The insect is dusted with pollen and this enhances pollination. The fruit are tiny brown capsules, and hang from the branch on a soft curved stem.

Distribution – This is a species of eastern North America which extends south to Georgia

! *Not recommended for eating*

Bog laurel in bloom at Pistolet Bay Provincial Park near Raleigh, Newfoundland, in mid July.

Bog laurel
Kalmia polifolia Wang.

In the past bog laurel leaves were dried and powdered and mixed with lard to apply to cold sores and other eruptions of the skin.

 The leaves are toxic to humans and domestic animals if taken internally.

Bog laurel's flowers grow on stiff upright ➤ stems which arise from the tips of branches.

▲
Bog laurel fruit turns red in late summer. It often persist through the winter, and sometimes still stands in spring as the new year's buds open.

Identification – The flowers are like those of sheep laurel but this shrub is quite short and grows on peatlands. It has shiny, dark green leaves in pairs on the stem. The midvein of each leaf is sunken and the leaves are whitened beneath. The flowers grow on the tips of the branches ('terminal'), and the fruit (larger than those of lambkill, and a nice clear red) grow on stiff, erect spikes at or near the tips of the branches.

Distribution – A species of cooler parts of North America which extends south to Colorado in the west and Pennsylvania in the east.

Larix

Larch
Larix laricina (DuRoi) K. Koch

Cone with young needles. ➤

Also called tamarack and hackmatack, and in Newfoundland commonly called 'juniper'. Alexander Robertson, a forester, tells me than in British naval documents of the seventeenth century there are frequent references to the use of juniper for masts, spars, etc. This seems likely to be the origin of the Newfoundland use of the name (see also *The Dictionary of Newfoundland English*, Toronto 1982/1990:282). The sap has long been used to promote clotting in open wounds. The roots were used for sewing seams of birch bark canoes, and the wood is dense, highly water-resistent, and excellent for building. The trunks are often curved upwards from the root so they are naturally shaped to follow the curve of the hull of a ship, and for this reason are frequently used to make the ship's 'knees'.

Identification – Most conifers are evergreen but this one is deciduous. In the autumn, the needles turn a lovely yellow, which is sometimes peachy in hue, and then they drop. Can be recognized by its lovely orangey-yellow foliage in the fall and by its very pale, often almost translucent, green needles in the spring. Most abundant on the edges of woods. Grows happily in wet ground along the edges of peatlands. There are two types of branches; short stubby ones and long ones. The cones are short and similar to those of spruce. Distribution – A tree of boreal North America, it is found from Alaska to Newfoundland and south into the northern of the eastern United States.

Larch in its fall dress. ➤

Its leaves and bark were used by Aboriginal peoples to produce medicinal teas and poultices with the same properties as the other evergreens of the same family. The crushed leaves were also used in steam baths and as a medicinal smudge. In Northern Europe, larch was considered a "preventative against enchantment, the smoke from burning larch was thought to drive away evil spirits, and parents had children wear collars of larch bark as a protection against the evil eye" (Lust, 1974: 597) The smoke is rich and pungent. Use the crushed leaves, fresh or dried, or the finely shredded bark. (Guédon)

In spring, young shoots and the inner bark can be boiled and eaten; these are rich in vitamins. The inner bark can also be dried and pounded into a flour, which can be added to wheat flour to stretch supply out. This is generally considered emergency food.

Inset: New needles of larch are like tiny shaving brushes.

Mature cones in August.

Lathyrus

Beach pea
Lathyrus maritimus Bigel.

▲ Ripe beach pea at L'Anse aux Meadows.

The leaves and seeds have traditionally been used as food and shipwrecked sailors have recovered from scurvy on a diet of the leaves.

Identification – These resemble sprawling garden peas with lovely burgundy-coloured flowers.

Distribution – Beach Pea grows on the shores around the northern Atlantic and Pacific Oceans and inland on the beaches of the Great Lakes of North America.

The most productive local member of the pea family is *Lathyrus maritimus*, the beach pea. As its name suggests, this pea grows on beaches, particularly at their upper margin a little above high-tide line – what in Newfoundland is often referred to as the 'landwash'. Beach pea seems to be as comfortable on coarse gravel as it is on sand.

I have had best success harvesting these while they are still green, rather than waiting for the pods to dry; the seeds are very hard, and even prolonged soaking, or boiling and soaking, does little to improve their texture. The green pods can be thrown into boiling water along with other beach plants - yellow mountain saxifrage (locally known as 'cabbage'), *Mertensia maritima* (oyster-leaf), and beach plantain, to make a fine wild soup. (MK)

▲ Beach pea pods. These were growing in the shelter of low bushes along a path at Cape Onion. They are much nicer to eat a little earlier in the season, while the pods are still soft and green.

Blooms of beach pea.

Caribou lichen, reindeer moss
Cladonia rangiferina

Cladonia growing on a rock. ➤

Lichens are generally safe to eat, though not pleasant. Those of our region should be soaked overnight (two or three changes of water recommended), and then crushed to make a powder which can be added to other flours to extend them. The flour can also be used to thicken soups and stews.

This type of *cladonia* is commonly known as 'British Soldiers' for its red coat.
▾

Caribou lichen is common in northern bogland and (as its name suggests) is a major food for caribou, which depend on it particularly in the winter. Here the main companion is blueberry.

At Fishing Point, St. Anthony, a beautiful butterfly rests amid caribou moss and a *Vaccinium*, probably tundra bilberry.

Ligusticum

In the Hebrides and other coastal parts of Scotland, this plant is used as a potherb and as a substitute for celery. It has a pronounced celery-like taste (milder after cooking; delicious cooked with beach plantain and dandelion greens) and makes a pleasant nibble while hiking along the coast.

Right and Below: These examples I photographed at ► Bird Cove, where they grow on rocky ground just above the high-tide mark.

Identification – The leaves are tough in nature and a dark green, and look like those of celery. The flat-topped flower clusters, followed by dry fruit, are distinctive.

Distribution – Scotch Lovage grows on coastal cliffs and beaches around the northern Pacific Ocean and northern Atlantic Ocean (northern Europe, Iceland, Greenland, and south to New York in North America).

▲
Fine Scotch lovage along the shore of the bay near St. Julian's (not far from Main Brook).

The leaves of lovage were added to tobacco smoking mixture by the Aboriginal people in western Canada. According to Nancy Turner (1978, vol. 2:98-99) "the root [...] was a valuable smoking condiment of the Shuswap, Kootenay, and Southern Okanagan Indian. A few pieces mixed with tobacco, in cigarette or pipes, is said to give the smoke a pleasant menthol taste and to act as relaxant." Another related species (*L. verticillatum*) was used in the same way by the Flathead Salish and Kootenay Indians in Montana (Turner [a]1978, vol. 2:98). Among such people as the Okanagan, it found an important role as a ceremonial medicine. The roots were burned and the smoke used to revive singers from a trance, and to help a person under the influence of the "Blue Jay spirit" or "taken " by spirits, and generally to alleviate unconsciousness, (Moerman, 1998:306; Turner, 1983:64). In the Prairies, the Crow people among others would add shavings of licorice root to tobacco, or sprinkled them on hot stones. (Guédon)

▲ Scotch lovage often grows just above the high-tide mark. The shores of Bonne Bay in Gros Morne Park (here with the Tablelands) provide excellent habitat.

Oysterleaf (leaves throughout; buds to left and at bottom center) growing together with silverweed whose fruit is at center.

Mertensia

Oysterleaf, sea lungwort
Mertensia maritima (L.) S.F. Gray

This is a strand plant; a plant that grows in circular patterns on the beach. It forms a round mat with blue flowers throughout the summer. Found at the upper fringes of beaches; prefers sand, coarse gravel.

◄ *Mertensia* detail.

The leaves make an interesting addition to salads through spring and summer, and are very good boiled or steamed with other wild beacfh greens.

Oysterleaf is eaten by the Inuit in Alaska, and considered a medicine against arthritis and bruises by the people in Saint Pierre et Miquelon islands. (Fleurbec, 1985:66-667) (Guédon).

Oysterleaf in a dominant ➤ position tends towards a circular growth pattern.

Identification – The sprawling stems have oval leaves that taper to each end and are a bluish colour because of a coating of tiny flakes of wax. The flowers are blue and tubular. It is a plant of the beach which is distinctive and easily told from its neighbours.

Distribution – Sea lungwort grows around the arctic oceans. It is found on beaches around northern North America from Maine to British Columbia and around Greenland, Europe, and Asia.

The flower and the pink buds at center near the top are oysterleaf; the tiny clusters of pinkish-green flowers are smooth orache. The larger flower head at center (its petals are gone – we see just the calyx) is locally called 'cabbage' and is gathered in summer for use in soups and stews. Its botanical name is *Honkenya peploides*.

Open space woods like this at the base of Aunt Bride's Hill, Gunner's Cove, offer ideal habitat for one-flowered wintergreen.

Moneses

This plant has a long history of medicinal use. The Montagnais, for example, steeped it to make a medicine for paralysis, and called it "the plant of four seasons". The fresh leaves are still used by Aboriginal people and European immigrants as an aromatic and strengthening substitute for tea, or chewed to keep teeth clean and breath fresh. A Main Brook resident (Ms Barbara Genge of Tuckamore Lodge) identifies this as the fruit used locally to make crème de menthe liqueur.

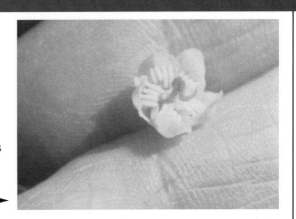

The complex 'face' of the flower will soon be ➤ replaced by the single green fruit.

Identification – A small plant with a rosette of evergreen leaves and a single white flower that nods in the cool boreal woods where it grows. The flower is faintly fragrant, white or rose-coloured, and looks both waxy and succulent. It can be confused, when not in flower, with some of the other wintergreens in the genus Pyrola

Distribution – It is circumboreal and grows in cooler parts of North America from Alaska to Newfoundland and south through the mountains in the west and east.

This is the most common view of the one-flowered wintergreen, its five-pointed fleshy star turned face-down.

Monotropa

Indian pipe
Monotropa uniflora L.

It has many common names like ice plant and corpse plant but convulsion root refers to its use in the treatment of nervous restlessness, convulsions, spasms, and fits. A diluted solution of sap has been used by a number of peoples for sore eyes.

◄ Ripe fruit at Bird Cove in August. A pocket tape recorder indicates the scale.

Identification – This ghostly plant of the cool woods is translucent white when growing and then it dries black. It has bracts along the stem and a single nodding cylindrical flower which straightens in fruit so that the seeds are effectively dispersed. It derives its nutrients from decaying organic matter of the duff on the forest floor.

Distribution – It occurs in Asia and from Alaska to Newfoundland and south, in the west, to Central America.

Seed pod in late fall, after the seeds have ➤ been dispersed.

yrica

Sweet gale
Myrica gale L.

From Bjornsson's Icelandic manuscript of 1475: "Its fragrance counteracts shooting pain in the head...crushed it dries boils. The juice of sweet gale dries matter in the ears and kills their worms. Small sweet gale is good for flux of blood and other purgation. Oil of sweet gale gives the hair strength to grow more."

Mature male flower buds in early fall. ➤

Identification – This is a very common shrub of wet places that has aromatic leaves and fruit. The leaves are a dull green, toothed at the tip, and are broader at the tip and taper to the base. The male flowers are in a tiny green/gold cone, the female a miniature burgundy brush. The fruit are clusters of nutlets with sharp-looking points.

Distribution – Sweet gale grows from eastern Asia across northern North America to northern Europe. On this continent, it extends south to Oregon, Minnesota, and North Carolina.

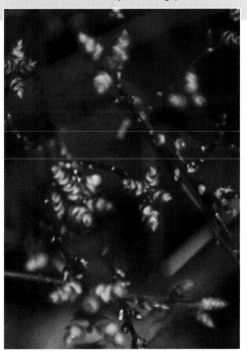

Sweet gale is an antiseptic and used to be made into a medicinal tea against all kinds of ailments. In Quebec, people used to place leaves of myrica in their bed sheets to give them a nice smell and to keep insects away (Frère Marie-Victorin, 1995:156). But it is equally useful and equally pleasant as a fumigant and at least one Aboriginal tribe, the Potawatomi, used to smudge with sweet gale to keep mosquitoes away. (Huron Smith, 1933:121).

The smoke is delightfully scented. Use the dried leaves, the miniature cone-like male buds, or the fruit. They can be lit directly on the sprig or thrown on the fire. (Guédon)

◄ Here male flowers of sweet gale have just begun to open.

A common plant in bogs and shallow pools. Abundant everywhere I have traveled in the Northern Peninsula and along the southern Labrador coast. Seems happiest along the drier edges of bogs, but can do very well even standing in 10 centimeters of water at the edges of ponds.

The leaves are very good for flavouring stews and soups (try one leaf per portion). The prickly-looking fruit and the male buds are particularly good crumbled on wild game. With small leaves, I use much as one uses bayleaf, but in the proportion 3 sweet gale to one leaf of bayleaf. On Bell Island (the more southerly of the Grey Islands east off the Northern Peninsula near Conche) I found a variety with leaves at least three times the size of the average I have seen elsewhere. (MK)

Myrica in late summer, near St. John's, By late summer the fruit is almost fully ripe, the leaves full-sized, and the buds almost ready for winter.

In spring the male flower cone ➤ opens, showing its golden interior, well before the leaves begin to show.

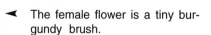

◄ The female flower is a tiny burgundy brush.

Myrica habitat in a shallow pond near the reconstructed sod houses at L'Anse aux Meadows in mid May.

Picea

White spruce	Black spruce
Picea glauca (Moench) Voss	*Picea mariana* (Mill.) B.S.P.

In her book on the use of plants for the past 500 years, Charlotte Erichsen-Brown quotes an old Icelandic author who wrote the following around 1475 : "Pinum is spruce. One shall take spruce (pine) cones and place upon coals and burn them somewhat, then one shall throw away the shell and clean the kernels and boil well in water... If one places these kernels just prepared upon the coals and draws to one's nose the smoke that come therefrom, that makes a man

happy and it moistens his body....if one cuts the bark of this tree during the winter time, a resin runs from it which he can use for incense... (Bjornnson 115, Larsen translation, in Erichsen-Brown, 1979:8)

Spruce bark, resin and leaves contain vitamin C; the Aboriginal people taught the European explorers arriving on the American Atlantic coast how to cure their sick crews of scurvy with decoctions of bark and needles. Spruce beer became a daily item in the diet of the colonists. Resin was used by the North American Indians as a poultice or bandage for open wounds, swellings and inflammations.

Spruce needles and resin produce a smoke with a strong balsamic component.
Use the twigs or leaves, fresh or dried. If fresh, place them on charcoal. If dried, they can burn by themselves. You can also use the resin itself. (Guédon)

Identification – Spruce has needles that are somewhat four-sided and that are attached on short spurs which can be seen on twigs which have lost their needles. The young twigs of White Spruce are smooth and pale in colour while those of Black Spruce are hairy and dark. The bark on older trunks is flaky
.

Distribution – - Both species grow across Canada and Alaska and south into the northern United States.

Spruce by Lookout Trail in Gros Morne Park.

"Spruce bread was made the same as the Hop bread only preparing the Spruce was a little different than preparing the hops. Small spruce branches [I would go for twigs!!] (were) put in the old iron pot (with water) and let it steep for about three to four hours. (The resulting liquid) was put in a large jar with three potatoes cut in small pieces. The potatoes made it work fast. After all this was done the jar was put away in a warm place for about three days until it worked. It was then ready for the flour." Dictionary of Newfoundland English (Toronto 1982/1990) 517-518. Recipe gives no quantities.

"Spruce beer: fermented drink made from an infusion of the boughs and 'buds' of the black spruce. ... The receipt for making it take as follows as Perfectly as I can get it. Take a copper that Contains 12 Gallons fill it as full of the Boughs of Black spruce as it will hold. Pressing them down pretty tight Fill it up with water Boil it till the Rind will strip off the Spruce Boughs which will waste it about one third take

them out and add to the water one Gallon of Melasses. Let the whole Boil until the Melasses are disolvd take a half hogshead & Put in nineteen Gallons of water and fill it up with the Essence. Work it with Barm and Beergrounds & in Less than a week it is fit to Drink."

Barm 'To make what we call Barm you'd boil your hops and then scrape some potato and then put a little bit of sugar on it. And you'd hang it up for to let it work.'
"To make what was called 'barm', one took a cup full of the grounds, added water and flour, stirred it well and wrapped it up warm [in a stone jar called a 'barm bottle'] and set it to rise." Ibid. 25 'Grounds' or 'beergrounds' seems to refer to a sort of sourdough. The Dictionary does not further explain it.

▲
Spruce (here probably black spruce) is a major feature of tuckamore, the dense growth along windy shores and steep, exposed slopes. Black spruce does better in wet soil (as here at St. Shott's on the Avalon Peninsula) than white spruce does.

Plantago

A seaside plant that grows by the beach and on rocky ledges of the seaside cliffs. It occasionally grows along roadsides where salt is spread in the winter.

Very pleasant to eat raw (salty, not strong tasting), excellent as an ingredient in salads and as a cooked vegetable, either steamed on its own or in combination with (for example) oysterleaf and smooth orache. It is sometimes called *Plantago juncoides* in books

Identification – The leaves look like green beans and the flower stalk resembles a lumpy rat's tail.

Distribution – It is a plant found around the sea coast of the Pacific and Atlantic Ocean.

Mature plants at Dildo Island.

◄ Beach plantain, shown here perched in the clefts of rock on the shore of Dildo Island, is even more at home on gravel or sand beaches.

Polygonum

Alpine smartweed
Polygonum viviparum L.

Several parts of this plant are used as a vegetable by northern peoples. The "roots" are starchy and have been eaten raw or cooked. The small bulbs ("bulbils") found in the inflorescence make a hiker's tasty treat .

Like most plants of the Burnt Cape, this is a very spare specimen of its species. ➤

◄ Alpine smartweed has a very pretty flower though it is inconspicuous. This is recommended (the flower stalk) as a trail nibble, as is the root stock, said to taste of almond.

Identification – The leaves, which are broadly oval in shape, are found in a tuft. The inflorescence is like a fine bottle brush; the lower flowers have been replaced by bulbils and the upper flowers are white to pink in colour

Distribution – The Alpine smartweed is found throughout northern Europe, Asia, and North America. It is found in Iceland and Greenland. In North America it is found from the Aleutian Islands to Newfoundland and through the mountains in the west to New Mexico and to New England in the east.

Potentilla

Silverweed
Potentilla anserina L

Silverweed was used in medicine for diarrhoea. The root was eaten either raw or cooked and is said to taste like parsnips. The root was also used as a source of red dye for wool and other cloths. Peterson (1977 70) recommends the roots for roasting, adding to soups and stews; or for boiling for 20 min., to be served with butter. Peterson says it tastes 'like parsnips or sweet potatoes'.

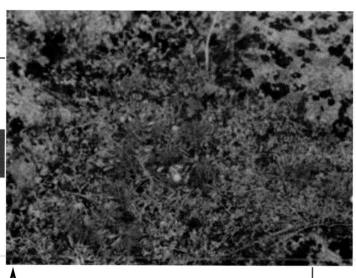

Silverweed buds on a lichen-covered rock.

◄Silverweed fruit.

Identification – This seaside plant is so pretty that it is often planted in gardens. It has a rosette of leaves with many leaflets that are toothed and covered with silvery-white hairs beneath. It produces runners like strawberries and spreads fairly quickly. The yellow flowers shine among the leaves. The common name is said to come from the silvery shine of the undersides of the leaves when they are blown by the wind.

Distribution – It occurs on beaches and other waterside habitats along both coasts of North America, across Canada, and Greenland, Iceland, Europe, and Asia.

Shrubby cinquefoil
Potentilla fruticosa L.

Some have made tea from the leaves (a handful of fresh leaves to a mug of boiling water - quite pleasant to drink MK) and early North Americans used it for bowel problems. It has risen to stardom in the horticultural world with many selections available.

Identification – A short shrub with hairy leaves that have five narrow leaflets. The twigs are much-branched and often are twisted. The flowers look like pale buttercups.

Distribution – A plant of cooler areas; it grows from Alaska to Newfoundland and south to New Mexico in the west and Pennsylvania in the east.

Λ
Early leaves of shrubby cinquefoil; near Side Pond Road ('the Burnover') near Roddickton.

Λ
A single flower of shrubby cinquefoil, past its best, on the Dog Peninsula near Bird Cove. In the left foreground is trailing juniper.

81

▲
Flowers of rough cinquefoil at the Burnt Cape.

Rough cinquefoil
Potentilla norvegica L.

The aboriginal people knew this plant and used it medicinally. The Chippewa chewed the roots and stems for a sore throat, and the Ojibwe used it as a general physic.

Identification – A rough cinquefoil has leaves that look like coarse strawberry leaves and it is up to half a metre tall. The flowers look like those of buttercups.

Distribution – This is a circumboreal species that is found through Asia, Europe, Iceland, Greenland, and across Canada and Alaska and south to Mexico in the west and North Carolina in the east.

This plant belongs to a family represented by more than three hundred species scattered throughout the northern hemisphere. This cinquefoil spans the whole circumpolar area (Frère Marie-Victorin, 1995 [1935]:340). It was occasionally used as a fumigant by the Navaho to alleviate venereal diseases. (Moerman 1998:435). (Guédon)

Marsh cinquefoil
Potentilla palustris (L.) Scop

This purple-flowered plant stands tall in the marshes. The root was used by the Chippewa and Ojibwe for dysentery and other stomach upsets.

Identification – - As the common name suggests, this cinquefoil is found in marshy places. It can be fairly tall in sheltered locations (about a half metre - though around L'Anse aux Meadows the average height is more like 10 cm.), has hairy leaves with five toothed leaflets, and red-purple flowers. A close look will show you the features in common with the rest of the group.

Distribution – This is a circumboreal species found across Asia, Europe, Iceland, Greenland, and North America from Newfoundland to Alaska and south to northern California in the west and Pennsylvania in the east..

▲
Detail of a fine marsh cinquefoil.

Marsh cinquefoil is very much at home along the footpaths crossing the land between the reconstructed sod houses and the modern village of L'Anse aux Meadows.
Inset: The bee is about one fourth the size of a mainland bumblebee.

There is another plant, *Sibbaldia* (*Sibbaldia procumbens*), which is quite uncommon and resembles this species. *Sibbaldia's* leaves are hairy, while this one's are smooth. The three-toothed cinquefoil is so common that it is often ignored but it is always worth checking just in case...

Identification – This is a common species of headlands and rocky barrens all across the island. It is a short plant with a rosette of shiny green evergreen leaves that have three leaflets, each with three teeth at the tips. There is a branched grouping of white flowers followed by dry brown capsules.

Distribution – It is found in Greenland and from Newfoundland to western Northwest Territories and south to Georgia in the east.

▲
Here is the tiny flower of Potentilla tridentata, three-toothed cinquefoil, together with some of last year's fruit.

▲
Here the leaves, with the three 'teeth' on the tip of each, show how pretty they can be.

Burnt cape cinquefoil
Potentilla usticapensis Fern.

There are a number of rare plants in Newfoundland, particularly on the west coast, because of the fascinating geological and glacial history of the island. This is one of those that is only found there.

Identification –A tiny plant with leaves that are densely covered in hair and have 3-5 leaflets which are attached along a stalk as in roses and dogberries. The flowers are a creamy colour.

Distribution – Named for Burnt Cape on the Northern Peninsula, its distribution is limited to there.

▲
A coin gives the scale of this tiny Potentilla.

 This plant is rare, and must not be disturbed for any purpose.

▲
Several small, yellow-flowered Potentillas grow on the Burnt Cape, an extremely stressful habitat. Of these, only the Burnt Cape cinquefoil is found on the Burnt Cape and nowhere else. Only a botanist can be certain which variety is which, *so when on the Burnt Cape, do not disturb the cinquefoils.*

Prunus

Pin cherry
Prunus pensylvanica L

The fruit are used for making jellies and there is a long tradition in North America for using the bark to make cough remedies. The leaves contain hydrogen cyanide and have been responsible for the death of many domestic animals

! *Deadly to many herbivores.*

Identification – This small tree is common in burnt-over areas that have the woods returning. The leaves are long, narrow, and glossy, and they turn a marvellous scarlet in the autumn. The clusters of white flowers, which have a lovely almond scent, are followed by scarlet fruit which have a large seed and a tart flavour.

Flowers and buds.

Distribution – This tree of the cooler woods is found from British Columbia to Newfoundland and south to Colorado in the west and North Carolina in the east.

Flowers and buds arise from the leaf axils.

Pyrola

The Wintergreen Family

Wintergreen and most of its close relatives contain salicine, the active ingredient in aspirin, which explains the use of its leaves (in teas and decoctions as well as poultices) and its berries in treating inflammations, pains, headaches, toothache, flu and colds, as well as fever. It is also used against asthma, late menstruations and kidney ailments. Wintergreen leaves were mixed with tobacco and smoked by the Woodland Indians, including the Cherokee people, the Ojibwa, the Chippewa and other tribes speaking an Algonkian language. Wintergreen has a very pleasant smell, spicy and resembling anise; this flavor is still present in the smoke, both sweet and pungent and is also a favorite flavor for scented candles. For smudging, use the dried shredded leaves.

▲
Pink pyrola at Burnt Cape.

Pink pyrola
Pyrola asarifolia Michx.

Aboriginal people had many uses for this species and its relatives. The Penobscot tribe combined this with six other ingredients to make a gonorrhea medicine.

◄ Flowers of *Pyrola asarifolia*.

Identification – There are a number of species which appear similar to this one. The leaves are round in outline, shiny, and leathery. The flowers are pretty, in their way, and have rose to pink petals.

Distribution – This species occurs in Asia and across North America from Alaska to Newfoundland and south to New Mexico in the west and to New England in the east.

Shinleaf
Pyrola elliptica Nutt.

It is always surprising how native plants were discovered to be effective for various ailments. This species and its relatives were used by aboriginal people for diseases of the breast, colds, wounds, eye ailments, weak nerves, and blisters. As well, the roots were boiled and drunk for weakness while the leaves were steeped to make a gargle for sores in the mouth.

Identification – This is a small evergreen plant of the woods which has elliptical leaves, as the latin name notes, and a wand of hanging, fragrant, creamy flowers.

Distribution – Shinleaf is found in Japan and in North America from British Columbia to Newfoundland and south to Pennsylvania in the east and New Mexico in the west.

◄ Pink pyrola growing out of a rotting log.

Lesser pyrola
Pyrola minor L.

Identification – The leaves are roundish in shape and have a matte surface. The margins have rounded teeth. The flowers are white to pink in colour.

Distribution – A circumboreal species found in Asia, northern Europe, Iceland, Greenland, and across North America from Newfoundland to Alaska and south to New England in the east and New Mexico in the west.

A number of species will often be lumped together by the casual lover of nature but then the botanist will toil endlessly to discern minute differences in the flowers, leaves, etc. The pyrolas have some differences in the shapes and textures of the leaves but in the flowers there are variations in the styles and stamens and other structures that help distinguish.

One-sided pyrola
Pyrola secunda L.

In rural England during earlier times, the leaves of pyrolas were used in poultices to be applied to bruises. Aboriginal people used this plant for rheumatism, coughs, and cankers.

Identification – Small plants of the woods with small oval, evergreen leaves. The wand of flowers arches and the white flowers hang down - from the lower (i.e. one) side. This is the only really distinctive pyrola that we have.

Distribution – This is the only species of pyrola which is common all across the province. It is circumboreal and found across Asia, northern Europe, Iceland, Greenland, and across northern Canada and Alaska and south in the west to Mexico and to Virginia in the east and New Mexico in the west.

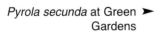

One-sided pyrola sampled from the base of St. Anthony Hill stairs.

Pyrola secunda at Green ➤ Gardens

Rhamnus

Alder-leaved buckthorn
Rhamnus alnifolia L'Her

Buckthorn has a long history of use and a reputation as the best and commonest plant laxative. The fruit have dramatic effects on the digestive tract; they are cathartic. Buckthorn is still listed in pharmacy references today and has few, if any, side effects. It was used on both sides of the Atlantic and, depending on the species, the berries or bark were used to prepare the potion. A tea made from the bark is particularly effective. Closely related to cascara.

Identification – This is a small shrub, usually about a metre tall. The leaves are quite distinctive in buckthorn. They are a sombre, dark green (much paler when new), and oval with fine teeth around the margin. The flowers are tiny greenish stars which are followed by black oval berries borne singly or in small clusters farther down on the branches. They are not considered edible because of their laxative qualities.

Buckthorn buds. These were taken in early June near Roddickton.

Distribution – Buckthorn grows in damp woods and thickets west of Gander on the island. It is found across southern Canada from British Columbia to the west coast of Newfoundland and south to Pennsylvania in the east and California in the west.

Buckthorn flower is dwarfed by its tiny new leaves.

Fully ripe buckthorn berries, September, near ➤ Roddickton.

A buckthorn thicket on Side Pond Road near Roddickton, August.

Rhododendron

▲ A typical globular cluster of flowers: a very small fly indicates the scale.

Identification – The leather-like green leaves which have the margins rolled under and the undersurface covered with rusty coloured velvety hairs make this plant easy to recognize (do not confuse it with the poisonous sheep laurel which is somewhat similar in appearance except for the undersides of its leaves which are green). There is a lovely cluster of white flowers in the early summer followed by plain brown dry capsules.

Distribution – It is found from Alaska to Greenland, across Canada and south to Pennsylvania.

This is the traditional camp tea of the north. The leaves are collected and steeped (never boiled or simmered!) and enjoyed around a camp fire. In the 19th century, powdered leaves were used as an insecticide and a tincture of the leaves was said to repel mosquitos.

▲ Flowers of Labrador tea, surrounded by fir.

▲ Buds of Labrador tea are said to have a delightful scent when crushed. It is, unfortunately, on a frequency I do not receive. (MK)

At Charlottetown, LAB, a few leaves still cling, and the buds for next year's growth tip each branch. In the background are spent fruit of willow.

Labrador tea was widely used as tea and for medicinal purposes by Aboriginal people and European voyageurs. Its anti-scorbutic properties have saved many lives among immigrant populations.

It is one of the alternative ingredients of the famous kinnikinnik smoking mixtures and can be smoked by itself, as well as smudged. Rhododendron (*Ledum palustre*), found in more northern regions, is more toxic than its cousin and is smudged by Sub-Arctic native people against mosquitoes, fleas, flies and other insects.

As a smudge it produces a sweet and pungent smoke. Use the dried leaves by themselves. They do not need any coal or support. Light the tips of the leaves. You can hold the twig while the leaves are burning. (Guédon)

Labrador tea grows here with balsam fir, spruce, and Kalmia.

For the tea, I have found the most pleasant result from leaves picked in early September and dried about ten days. It takes about thirty leaves to make a mug of tea - pour the boiling water over the leaves in the cup to avoid releasing toxins. This is the "tea" of the Innu "tea dolls" of Labrador - an excellent warming and energizing emergency drink. (MK)

At Burnt Cape a single flower, not a cluster, is all this stressed plant can raise.

In drier portions of bogland you will often find Labrador tea.

Ribes

Currants have traditionally been used to make jelly, jam, and cordial, and aboriginal people used the bark to make medicine for digestive upsets in people and domestic animals. The fruit are rich in vitamin C and so served well in northern climes.

Identification – We do not have the black and white striped article on the island but we do have a reasonable facsimile of its scent since most parts of the plant smell like a skunk when bruised. The branches of this short shrub do not have prickles and the leaves are typical of currants. The bristly red fruit are on drooping stalks.

Distribution – This is the most common currant in the province. It occurs in Alaska, across Canada, and south to North Carolina in the east.

◄ *Ribes glandulosum*, unripe fruit.

Flowers of skunk currant on a steep slope by the road overlooking Conche.

Skunk currant takes its common name from the scent of its leaves when you crush them. The fruit is covered with tiny hairs. These were photographed at Bird Cove.

Gooseberry can thrive even in spots that receive very little sun, as here on the fringe of a clearing.

Smooth gooseberry
Ribes hirtellum Michx.

Gooseberries are relished by all those who have access to them and aboriginal people often cooked them with corn. The berries were picked and dried for winter use. The roots were used for back pain, sore eyes, and uterine problems.

Identification – This shrub has scattered prickles on the branches. The leaves may or may not have hairs but the margins and leafstalks do have hairs. The white flowers are borne in clusters of 2-4 and they produce dark red or purplish fruit that are smooth and edible.

Distribution – It grows across Canada and south to North Dakota, Ohio, and Pennsylvania. It occurs throughout Newfoundland but has not been reported from Labrador.

Gooseberry fruit.

Bristly black currant
Ribes lacustre (Pers.) Poir.

Black currants have been used by many peoples to make jams and jellies for food and for therapeutic use. European colonists made cordials and wines from black currant and consumed them for their medicinal properties.

Unripe fruit of bristly black currant.
Inset: ripe fruit.

Identification – As the common name suggests, this shrub has bristles on the branches and fruit. The leaves have hairs around the margins. The flowers are on drooping stalks and are green, tinged with purple. The stalks and sepals of the flowers are covered with sticky hairs. The fruit are dark purple or black and edible.

Distribution – This currant is found across northern North America and extends south to California in the west and Tennessee in the east.

Bristly black currant is thoroughly at home in open woodland at Bird Cove.

Swampy red currant
Ribes triste Pallas

In addition to the use of the berries as food, the stems and roots were used by aboriginal people for health problems encountered by women. The stems and roots were also used for kidney stones and other problems of the urinary tract.

Identification – This short shrub has smooth branches and leaves that are usually smooth above and hairy beneath. The flowers are greenish-purple and the flower stalks have sticky hairs. The smooth, red fruit are edible.

Distribution – This is a boreal plant that grows in eastern Asia and across northern North America; south to Oregon and South Dakota in the west and Virginia in the east.

Ripe fruit of swampy red currant. ➤

Fruit of swampy red currant at Bird Cove.

Rosa

Northeastern rose
Rosa nitida Willd.

Rose flower.

Traditionally in North America the root and some other plant parts have been used to treat eye infections and the hips have been used for stomach disorders. The hips have also been used to make a preserve and for jelly and a particularly nice syrup and we now know that they are very rich in vitamin C.

Identification – This species is easily distinguished by the dense dark red bristles found on the younger stems, much as are found on a raspberry. The leaflets have toothing around the margin and almost to the base of the leaflet. The pink flowers are wonderfully fragrant and are followed by orange-red hips.

Distribution – This rose is found in northeastern North America from eastern Ontario to Newfoundland and south to New England. See also Virginian rose.

ROSE HIP SYRUP

Put rose hips in a pan and cover with water. Bring water to a boil, stirring occasionally. Simmer for 20 minutes. Strain. To the liquid, add about 1/3 to 1/2 the weight of sugar; bring just to the boil; store in sterilized jars. This syrup will keep for years.

◄ Hips of wild rose *(R. virginiana).*

Virginian rose
Rosa virginiana Mill.

A bud picked in the evening and put in a small vase will open in the morning and provide its wonderful perfume. The petals can be candied or used to make rose water, and the hips make good jam, jelly, or tea.

Identification – The stems of this shrub have scattered curved prickles. The leaflets have toothing but only on the upper three-quarters of the margins. The flowers often seem to be a paler pink than the northeastern rose.

Distribution – Occurs from southern Ontario to Newfoundland and south to Alabama.

Spent rose *(virginiana)* with buds.

Buds of wild rose *(R. virginiana)*.

In North America, rose petals have attracted the attention of aboriginal people for their sweet smell and are often used as perfume, hair and body wash, and cosmetics. Rose hips are everywhere picked and preserved as winter food. In eastern North America, the Aboriginal people, especially Cree and other Algonkian speakers, use roses, especially prickly rose (*R. acicularis*) as an all-purpose protection. Branches and a tea made from branches of prickly rose were brought in to protect people from bad spirits, sorcery, and ghosts.

Dried rose petals are not burnt by themselves but they have long been added to incense to increase its erotic appeal or its spiritual potency. (Guédon)

103

Rubus

Stemless plumboy
Rubus acaulis Michx.

Stemless plumboy fruit.

The fruit are rarely found in any abundance but are certainly a welcome treat. The flowers are pretty and an unusual colour to be encountered.

Identification – The plant's appearance is quite similar to that of bakeapple but the flowers are pink and the fruit is like the hairy plumboy's. It is a short plant and there is usually only one fruit.

Distribution – Found from Alaska to Labrador and south to Colorado in the west and to Newfoundland and the Gaspe in the east.

Bakeapple
Rubus chamaemorus L.

The berry has a distinctive taste and is craved by many. It is called cloudberry in Scandinavia (hjórtron in Sweden) and there it is made into a liqueur and preserves. Fruit set is often spotty because the flowers are killed by late spring frosts. Although picking is backbreaking work, the harvest is well worth it.

Identification – This plant just gets above the surface of the bog and produces two rough-looking maple-like leaves. May also be found growing taller among dwarf birches, where it ripens later than in more open areas. The berries often stand above the birches - the flower must be lifted to where pollinating insects can reach it. There are separate male and female plants and the white female flower is followed by a luscious warm yellow berry. This colour may be what gives it its common name.

Male flower of bakeapple

Distribution – This is a northern species found from Alaska across Canada in the northern or cooler parts of each province, in Greenland, and in northern Europe.

◄ A ripe bakeapple, translucent, on bog soil with mosses and crowberry.

BAKEAPPLE SWEET SAUCE

Fill your pan about 2/3 with bakeapples Heat slowly to slow boil. Add brown sugar (about 1/6 the weight of fruit). Boil about three minutes. Store in mason jars or freeze (e.g. in freezer bags).

Makes an excellent topping for ice cream.

A very successful pie fruit. Most distinctive flavour of the raspberry family - the fresh berry is an acquired taste. Bakeapples picked when newly ripe (before they go soft) can be quick-frozen on a cookie sheet and stored for individual use later.

Bakeapples nearing full ripeness along ► the Dog Peninsula (Bird Cove).

BAKEAPPLE CRUMBLE

1 c flour
1/2 c brown sugar
1 c rolled oats

1 tsp cinnamon
1/3 c shortening
3 c bakeapples

Combine flour, brown sugar, oats and cinnamon. Cut in shortening. Press half of mixture into greased pan. Spread with bakeapples. Cover with remaining crumbs and pat smooth. Bake at 350F for 30 minutes or until browned. If you wish, you can use a combination of bakeapples and blueberries, or bakeapples and raspberries, or one cup of each for pleasant variants.

Bakeapple pie at the Plum Point Motel. ►

Immature bakeapple berry.

Raspberry
Rubus idaeus L

In addition to many culinary uses, raspberries have served as medicines. The leaves have been steeped or powdered and used to help ease childbirth labour in women and domestic animals. Roots have been used for coughs, sore throats, chronic dysentery, piles, and gonorrhea.

In a single photo we can see a bud (above), an open ➤ flower, and, just to right of that, a fertilized ovary.

Identification – The raspberry has metre-tall canes that have leaves with 3-7 leaflets and that grow for two years. The first year canes are reddish and densely covered with bristles. The second year canes branch a bit at the tips and have white flowers followed by wonderful red thimble-like fruit.

Distribution – Raspberries are circumboreal and in North America they occur across Canada and south to northern Mexico in the west and to Tennessee in the east.

Raspberry fruit, eaten fresh, dried or preserved as jam, are a favorite food everywhere, for human beings as well as their largest furry relatives. In North America as in Europe, decoctions of leaves and roots are taken for various ailments, from boils and bellyache to gynaecological complaints, including childbirth pain, and for kidney troubles as well as for sores, colds, and coughs. (Guédon)

The leaves of raspberry, picked while small (even into the fall), provide a pleasant ingredient for wild salads. They may also be used to make a tea.

▲
The raspberry's flower is an unassuming white.

Ripe fruit in August, Bird Cove.

RASPBERRY·APPLE PIE

Pastry for 9-inch pie
2 c chopped apples
2 c raspberries
3/4 c brown sugar
1/2 tsp nutmeg

2 eggs or 6 tbsp oil
1 tbsp lemon juice
1 tbsp flour
1 tbsp butter or margarine

Line plate with pastry. Combine remaining ingredients except butter and mix well. Turn into pie plate. Dot with butter. Top with full crust or lattice. Bake at 375F for 45 minutes.

Stemmed plumboy, arctic plumboy
Rubus paracaulis Bailey

This species resembles a more widespread species that the Vikings would have known from their travels in northern climes. The fruit are not produced in abundance but they are tasty.

Identification – This species resembles the hairy plumboy except that it does not produce running stems and it has pink flowers

Distribution – The stemmed plumboy has a restricted distribution; found in central Alberta and Saskatchewan, northern Manitoba to northern Quebec, Labrador, and a few places in Newfoundland, New Brunswick, Nova Scotia, and the Gaspé.

A plumboy blossom opening.

These were photographed by the roadside in the village of L'Anse aux Meadows; they are also abundant near old root cellars nearby. I found a particularly rich harvest of these behind the gas station/restaurant farther south at Parson's Pond - which also has caribou and moose listed on the menu. I saw many of these in bloom along the road from the ferry at Blanc Sablon, Quebec, to Red Bay, Labrador; and the area from Roddickton to Main Brook and Conche has very rich pockets.

Arctic plumboy can thrive even where there is virtually no visible soil.

Salix

ASA tablets are universally known and used to ease pain. The key ingredient in these was originally derived from willow branches. Willows have also been useful because they have long flexible branches that are ideally suited for weaving into baskets, carpets, etc. Willow leaves (as boiled vegetable) are an important element of the diet of people living above the Arctic Circle: they are a good source of vitamins.

▲
This wattle fence protects a vegetable garden at Ferryland, the colony of Lord Baltimore on the Avalon Peninsula. The taller varieties of willow growing in the Northern Peninsula could have served similar purposes.

Identification – Willows are easily distinguished from other woody plants because the buds along the twigs are covered by one scale whereas other species have a number of bud scales. The catkins are structures containing the flowers. The sexes are found on separate shrubs.

Distribution – Damp places are the natural habitat of these shrubs and trees. There is a number of dwarf species found on headlands and in the north, and many shrubs and trees along streams and rivers. Salix is found throughout the world except in Australia.

Pussy willow
Salix discolor Muhl

◄ Male catkins of
pussy willow
growing in wet
ground on the
margin of woods
at Roddickton.

Female catkins ➤ of Canada willow, one of the few (small) tree-sized willows in our area, in early spring.

Silverleaf willow
Salix argyrocarpa Anderss.

Silverleaf (or sil- ➤
verfruited) willow
plant.

Canada willow
Salix brachycarpa Nutt.

◄ Catkins in early
spring.

Ungava willow
Salix cardifolia Pursh

Salix cardifolia ➤
'with heart-
shaped leaves'.

Grey willow
Salix glauca L.

Two views of
female flowers
of grey willow
on the Burnt
Cape.

115

Netvein dwarf willow, netted willow
Salix reticulata L.

Male catkins of
netvein willow.

Female catkins
of netvein wil-
low at Round
Head, L'Anse
aux Meadows.

Bearberry dwarf willow
Salix uva-ursi Pursh

Bearberry wil-
low in early
spring. ➤

Waghorn's willow, roundleaf willow
Salix vestita Pursh

◄ A dime shows
the scale of this
roundleaf willow
at the Burnt
Cape.

Salix sp., female flower

Many willows cannot be identified
certainly by photographs alone.
The sexes are on separate plants.

Salix sp., male flower ➤

Here dogberry blooms in mid May along Cook's Harbour Road, near the old St. Anthony airport.

Streptopus

Twisted-stalk, white mandarin
Streptopus amplexifolius

Very closely related to the following species.

Peterson (1977:148) recommends the young shoots as a trail nibble and for addition to salads. He recommends caution in eating the berries, as they can be cathartic.

This close cousin of *S. roseus* has a darker flower (purplish); and its fruit is more orange.

Identification – Like rose twisted-stalk in overall appearance; but has leaves with heart-shaped bases and the nodes are hairless. Its flowers start out pale green, and turn pale purple as they mature. Its fruit are more orange, rather than rose twisted-stalk's striking red.

Distribution – Range more restricted than rose twisted-stalk , not found as far west.

Pale flowers of rose twisted-stalk at Roddicton, early June. It is very difficult to distinguish it from its sister twisted-stalk.

Identification – The plants are very pretty. They have upright stems and oval leaves along the stems, much like Solomon's Seal. There are two species on the Island: this one has leaves that taper to the base and the node where they attach is hairy.

Distribution – This species is found across the island but more commonly in central and western portions. It is found across boreal Canada and Alaska and south to Oregon in the west and Georgia in the east.

The fruit look luscious and are eaten by some people but they are cathartic so caution is required. It is more nourishing than tasty (has a flavour somewhat reminiscent of cucumber), and probably should be considered a survival food. It is found most easily in open woods (the Fox Farm hill at St. Anthony has an abundance). The fruit are some of the most attractive of the lot.

Erichsen-Brown reports that native Americans used the fruit for coughs and kidney problems.

Ripe fruit of rose twisted-stalk on a bright September day.

Brilliant red ripe fruit ➤
of *Streptopus roseus*
explain its botanical
name.

◄ Green fruit: as for the
flower, the stem attaches
at the leaf axil, but below
the leaf.

Rose twisted-stalk is the pink flower at the lower left, here growing with Clintonia.

Tussilago

Coltsfoot
Tussilago farfara

Coltsfoot is a very hardy member of the family of the Composita. When you first spot it in the spring, with its bright yellow flower full open, it looks for all the world like a dandelion that has forgotten to put up its leaves. On closer inspection, you see that the stems are pale brown, not green; and that they have a scaly appearance.

The leaves of coltsfoot give it its English name. After it has finished blooming the scaled flower stalks wither and only the distinctive leaves remain above ground to identify it.

Coltsfoot in full bloom. The flower has a central dome (which reminds MK of a 'punk dandelion'!) surrounded by radiating outer petals.

Identification – Coltsfoot leaves do not appear until the flower is turning white – again resembling dandelion with its fly-away 'parachuted' seeds – and they are nothing at all like the dandelion leaf, or the leaf of any of the hawkweeds whose flowers it also resembles. It is the leaves that give coltsfoot its common name: they are shaped somewhat like the colt's footprint, and about the right size. Once you have seen the leaf, this plant is immediately recognizable at all its growth stages.

Distribution – Eastern Canada and U.S. south to Minnesota and New Jersey.

Coltsfoot has long been used to make a spring tonic (it has a great deal of vitamin C, vitamin A, and other important nutrients likely to have been in short supply over winter). The young leaves can be used in salads or steamed for a few minutes. The flower buds also can be steamed or boiled and eaten. The leaves can be used as a salt substitute: put them in a frying pan over a low flame and dry them out. Powder the dried leaf and sprinkle it as you would sprinkle salt. The dried leaves can be steeped to make a tea.

Fresh leaves can be boiled with a little honey or sugar to make a cough syrup; or, with more sugar and longer cooking, a candy/cough drop.

132

Coltsfoot dominates a scree slope near woody Point in Gros Morne Park, late May.

Urtica

Stinging nettle is not found in Newfoundland earlier than AD 1000. There is a possibility the Norse introduced it, but it may have come in later.

Stinging nettle loses its sting when cooked. Pick small upper leaves in summer (wear gloves!). In early spring, the whole shoot is edible.

Wearing gloves is a good idea when harvesting. The young leaves and the very young shoots can be steamed or boiled; the resulting stock is an excellent soup base and can also be drunk as a tea. Some prefer to discard the cooked plant; others eat it in the soup or with butter as cooked vegetable.

Identification – *The stinging nettle can be a handsome plant, with the purple veining and often purplish leaf bases. In our area it can grow to about a metre high, though it rarely attains that height. The leaves are coarsely toothed and roughly heart-shaped. The tiny greenish flowers are in the leaf axils. The whole is covered with tiny, bristly hairs which, when broken inject an irritant (formic acid - the same chemical as used by ants) into the skin. The mechanism used to bring this about is a botanical marvel.*

Distribution –*Much of Canada and the U.S. south to Illinois and Virginia.*

Blueberry flowers in a particularly rich patch at Cuckold's Cove by Signal Hill, st. John's.

Cranberry
Vaccinium macrocarpon Ait.

Ripe large cranberries at Bird Cove in early September.

'Cranberry' comes from 'crane-berry' since the flowers look like nodding cranes. The fruit are acid in nature and aboriginal people used them for stomach and other problems and applied crushed fruit to wounds and sores.

The nodding pink flower of the large cranberry usually stands tall over the trailing stems.

The Aboriginal people used the leaves for a diuretic and tonic tea. They also mixed the leaves with tobacco or added them to their kinnikinnik smoking mix. The flavour is rather mild. For smudging, use the dried and shredded leaves. (Guédon)

Identification – The cranberry can be distinguished from the marshberry (Vaccinium oxcoccos) by a number of characters: the leaves are about the same width throughout their length, there is a leafy stem extending beyond the flowers or fruit, the flower and fruit stalks have a pair of tiny leaves just below the flowers or fruit (i.e. above the middle), and the fruit tend to be spherical.

Distribution – This species is found from Minnesota to Newfoundland and south to North Carolina. It is usually found near the ocean.

◄ This unripe cran-
berry clearly shows
the stem arising
behind the last
sprig of leaf.

Green cranberries at Cape Spear. The large cranberry is ➤
much less common than the marshberry on the Northern
Peninsula.

▲
Ripe cranberries rest on their own leaves at Bird Cove.

◄ In this picture we see one tiny newly-formed fruit (just right of center), just above it a larger green fruit, and many berries nearing ripeness. The larger leaves belong to three-toothed cinquefoil.

CRANBERRY BREAD

1/4 c shortening	1/2 c sugar
2 c flour	2 tsp baking powder
1/2 tsp soda	1 tsp salt
3/4 c orange juice	1 tbsp grated orange rind
1 c cranberries	2 eggs or 4 to 6 tbsp oil

Cream shortening, sugar, and eggs. Add dry ingredients, juice and cranberries. Bake in loaf pan 1 hr. at 350F.

Here a penny gives the scale of the large cranberry close to fully ripe.

Marshberry, small cranberry (Swedish tranbär.)
Vaccinium oxycoccos L. Also *V. microcarpon*

'*Oxycoccos*' means "sour berry" which is an apt descriptor. Aboriginal people used to cook these with maple sugar or honey and they are still enjoyed today. They are eaten by residents wherever they occur.

▲ Ripe marshberries at Bird Cove, September.

◄ Ripe marshberries at Bird Cove. Note the tear-drop shape in the berries at far right. The larger leaves in the upper left corner are sweet gale.

Identification – The marshberry is a trailing evergreen with slender stems. It differs from the cranberry in having oval leaves (broader at the base), the flowers and fruit are borne at the tips of the stems with no shoots beyond them, and the pair of small leaves on the flower and fruit stalks are near or below the middle of the stalk. The fruit are often oval-shaped and, when unripe, are beige mottled with brown.

Distribution – A wide-ranging species with a circumboreal range through Asia, Europe, Iceland, Greenland, and across northern North America. It extends south to Oregon in the west and North Carolina in the east.

These small cranberries have the same qualities as their larger cousin, and are used in exactly the same ways.

▲ Two flowers of *V. oxycoccos* with bog mosses, crowberry, and roundleaf sundew.

A marshberry flower bud stands above the bog mosses it grows in. ➤

Last year's berry, still sweet but easily squashed (or 'squat' as locals say) with crowberry and lichens. It can tolerate very damp conditions, as here at L'Anse aux Meadows. ▼

▲ A family group gathers marshberries on a bog near Ste. Barbe, not far from the Labrador ferry terminal.

143

Alpine bilberry, tundra bilberry (Swedish odon)
Vaccinium uliginosum L.

In 1892, Mr. Millspaugh said that the wine made from the fruit of this plant is a narcotic and very intoxicating. The fruit can also be boiled into a paste and dried to make a vegetal pemmican or what might be called fruit leather today.

Use as you use blueberry.

◄Flowers of tundra bilberry, though similar in form to blueberry's, are a lovely greenish cream colour.

Ripe fruit of tundra bilberry are ➤ generally smaller than those of blueberry, and a paler blue.

Identification – *This shrub usually grows in cool, windy habitats so it hugs the ground. The leaves are oval and widest towards the tip. They are a dull green and often appear whitish. They have no teeth on the margin. The fruit resemble those of blueberry but tend to be flattened at the tip and do not have a prominent little crown.*

Distribution – *This is a very northern species that grows across northern Asia and Europe,* *Iceland, Greenland and across the northern boreal of North America, south to northern California in the west and Vermont in the east. I have seen it most abundant, in our region, on the top of St. Anthony hill (the new walkway from Fishing Point road makes this more accessible) and on the highland which stretches from there to Goose Cove.*

'Partridgeberry' is a local name. The berries are sweetest after they have been frozen: they are then called 'springberries' (even in September!), and are tricky to harvest, as there is simply a thickish membrane around a liquid core. This is called lingonberry in Scandinavia, and mountain cranberry in eastern North America. It is called redberry in Labrador and in the Northern Peninsula but this is not much help as the name 'redberry' is commonly used to cover all of the low-growing red fruits of the region. This simplifies harvest. Fortunately none of the local low-growing red berries is toxic to humans. There is one poisonous red berry, *Actaea*, which grows in the region; but its stalk is quite tall – often a metre or more – and its berries on their stiff stems make a loose scarlet globe. There is also a white-berried *Actaea* which is equally poisonous.

Ripe partridgeberries

Identification – This can be confused with a number of species. It generally forms a small patch (about a foot across). The leaves have no teeth, the margins are about parallel, the upper surface is glossy and the midrib is furrowed, and the lower surface is pale with dark bristles. The flowers are rosy bells and the fruit are shiny, burgundy-red berries.

Distribution – This northern species is found across northern Asia and Europe, Iceland, Greenland, across boreal Canada and south to New England.

Here we see partridgeberries growing comfortably along with crowberry.

A ground-hugger, found very commonly along the drier edges of bogs. Survives well (though less dependably for fruiting) in exposed rocky places - the top of Micky's Hill near the lookoff, Fishing Point at St. Anthony and the crest of Fox Farm hill; on Round Head hill at L'Anse aux Meadows; on the lower slopes of the Burnt Cape at Raleigh; in the woods around Charlottetown, LAB. The berries can survive the winter under snow, and are sweetest and juiciest - though tricky to harvest as the skins are very soft and the interior liquid - as the snow clears in spring. Found in similar locations throughout the Northern Peninsula: the heaviest-bearing I have seen were in open woods in the park at Hawkes Bay.

◄Partridgeberry flowers and buds can often be found together on a single plant. The companions here are crowberry and another *Vaccinium*, probably tundra bilberry.

Flowers of partridgeberry bloom ► here at different stages along with crowberry (sprigs) and one lonely cranberry flower (top). There are leaves of another *Vaccinium* (tundra bilberry?) in the foreground, the whole growing in wet bog mosses.

The fruit has many culinary uses. In earlier times partridgeberries were preserved in barrels of water in a cellar. Their acidity prevented spoiling. The leaves were used by the Shakers for urinary tract problems.

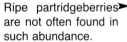

Ripe partridgeberries are not often found in such abundance.

◄ Partridgeberry cheesecake is one of the most interesting desserts at the Plum Point Motel restaurant.

Jam: I like sugar to about half the weight of cooked berries. Apple cooked with them, or Certo, gives a thicker consistency. May be substituted for cranberry in recipes. Also makes great wine. (MK)

PARTRIDGEBERRY CAKE

1/2 c shortening
1 c brown sugar
3 tbsp oil
1/2 tsp vanilla
1 3/4 c flour

2 tsp baking powder
1/4 tsp salt
3/4 c milk
1 1/2 c partridgeberries

Cream shortening and sugar together until light and fluffy. Add oil and beat thoroughly. Add vanilla. Put flour into a large bowl, and add baking powder and salt. Add dry ingredients to creamed mixture, adding a little of the milk each time. Fold in partridgeberries. Pour into greased pan (8-inch square should do it). Sprinkle with a little brown sugar. Bake 45 to 50 minutes in moderate oven (350F).

Viburnum

Northern wild raisin
Viburnum cassinoides L.

This is not common in the Northern Peninsula, but is found occasionally in sheltered spots. 'Northern', after all, is a comparative term. The fruit taste somewhat like prunes and, eaten in quantity, have similar effects. This is the shrub of choice for local dowsing-rods. One dowser said that this shrub will usually grow over ground water and casual observation would seem to confirm this.

Identification –This wonderful shrub is attractive in all seasons. The winter twigs have long, narrow, scurfy brown winter buds in pairs. The shiny leaves are in pairs on the stems and have a smooth to slightly toothed margin. They turn scarlet in the autumn. The flowers are in mounds of creamy white and the fruit turn from cream to reddish to dark purple.

Distribution – A species of eastern North America. It is found from Ontario to Newfoundland and south to Alabama.

Terminal clusters of uniform small white flowers and its long, pointed, rather narrow leaf make this easy to distinguish from its cousins the squashberry and the highbush cranberry.

The dark fruit grow in clusters – a likely reason for the 'raisin' in the common name.

This is a delight available to those who frequent the northern woods. Its flavour is just right to use as a condiment for game. The large seed dictates that a jelly be made in preference to jam or preserves. A really delightful 'spread' is now being marketed by a St. Lunaire company. I (MK) find that, if you eat the berries hot, the seed is almost undetectable - it works astoundingly well in scones or biscuits, but you must eat them hot. Bears, too, are fond of squashberries.

These ripe berries, on a typical background of green squashberry leaves, I photographed at Micky's Hill in Griquet/St. Lunaire. (MK)

The white petals drop when the flower has been fertilized, and the fertilized ovaries soon form the green berries.

Identification – *The leaves have three lobes and coarse toothing. They turn dark red or purplish in the autumn. The flowers are white and in clusters that arise from leaf joints lower on the stems. The fruit are a clear red and have a large flat seed.*

Distribution – *It is found in the boreal regions of North America from Alaska to Newfoundland and south to Colorado in the west and to Pennsylvania in the east. It is quite common on the island and is found in Labrador.*

Squashberry likes disturbed areas (near new roads, along walking trails), open woods. I have seen these at L'Anse aux Meadows; Griquet/St Lunaire (Micky's Hill); on the Fox Farm Hill at St. Anthony (also known as Tea House Hill, up behind the hospital); at the campground in Pistolet Bay Provincial Park; at Plum Point/Bird Cove; in woods along the shores of Ten Mile Lake; in sheltered places between boulders along Philips Garden walk at Port au Choix; in the park along the river at Hawkes Bay. They are common in parts of Gros Morne Park. In our region, generally low-growing (seldom more than 2 m. high; and moose browse on them, keeping them much lower than that). The best yield is found where they are protected from browsing - islands in sheltered bays and the like. The bark has been dried and shredded for use as a minor ingredient in smoking mixtures. (Guédon)

Squashberry flowers grow in clusters at the leaf axils.

Young fruit.

The dark red leaves of this squashberry at Ten Mile Lake (near Plum Point/Bird Cove) result from soil chemistry, not from a difference of species. Squashberry ripens in late August/early September.

MOOSE STEW WITH SQUASHBERRIES

I find a Dutch oven the most efficient cook-pot for this.

Take equal weights of moose meat, onion, and squashberries. Potato, carrot, turnip, parsnip if you like it - quantity in proportion to the meat.

Brown the meat. Add onion and cook a few minutes. Add squashberries, cover, place in oven preheated to 350-375F. The time required for cooking depends entirely on the weight of meat cooked; 2h 30 mins. will be about enough for two pounds' weight.

Add the cut-up vegetables for just enough time to cook them. I like them in fair sized pieces (large enough that I can identify the vegetable before putting it in my mouth), which means they must go in for about the last half-hour of cooking.

Squashberry thrives in open woodland, especially on the fringe of clearings.

◄ Squashberry buds open after the leaves are fully open but before they reach full size.

These opening squash-berry buds and flowers were at the foot of the walk up Tea House Hill at St. Anthony in July. ➤

Highbush cranberry
Viburnum trilobum Marsh.

This lovely shrub holds its fruit until well into the winter and the berry flavour is enhanced by frost. Traditionally, the berries have been used for swollen glands and the bark has been used to make a tea which was drunk for urinary tract problems, asthma, leg cramps, and hysteria.

For smudging, use the peeled and dried stems or the dried leaves. (Guédon)

The large outer 'flowers' have no reproductive function other than to attract pollinating insects that hunt by sight.

In early July, these highbush cranberries bloom on the fringe of woodland along the road from Wiltondale to Lomond in Gros Morne Park. You can see the distinctive terminal clusters of flowers from a considerable distance.

Identification – The leaves are similar to those of Squashberry but are often not so rounded in the lower half of the blade. The white flowers are borne on the tips of the stems and have a cluster of smaller flowers surrounded by a ring of larger flowers which look like those of hydrangea. The fruit are a clear red and have a large flat seed.

Distribution – This is not common and is not found near the coast. It is reported from the‹ Northern Peninsula but is probably found deep in the woods. I found these flowers along the road to Lomond in Gros Morne Park.

Their position on the ends ➤
of the twigs ('terminal')
makes ripe highbush cran-
berries easy to spot in
winter.

◄ Ripe highbush cranberries
against a winter sky.

Fauna

Introduction

The Viking settlement at L'Anse aux Meadows is on the northern tip of the Great Northern Peninsula of Newfoundland, on the lower of two terraces on the shore of Épaves Bay. The Labrador Current, which brings very cold water down from the high arctic, splits near here, sending one branch down the Strait of Belle Isle towards the Gulf of St. Lawrence, the other, larger, to the east and south.

Épaves bay is shallow, rocky, and exposed to the sea unlike many of the fjords where other Viking settlements were located. There are islands just outside the bay which give it some shelter, but if the wind is coming from west or northwest, sailing ships must have extreme difficulty leaving the bay. This site has not been chosen on the basis of its poorly sheltered harbour. The photograph [below] is surely an indicator: you can see your neighbours coming by sea long enough ahead of their arrival that you can prepare for them.

Farther south along the west coast of the Northern Peninsula, in the region now consecrated as an Unesco World Heritage Site, Gros Morne National Park, there are fjords and deep sheltered bays. Closer at hand along the east coast of the Northern Peninsula there are marvellous fjords, those at Great Harbour Deep and Little Harbour Deep being the closest to L'Anse aux Meadows. If the Norse explored as far south as this, the similarities to their Scandinavian homelands (particularly Norway) may well have drawn them to settle here. Changes in sea level over the past millennium, unfortunately, make looking for such theoretical settlements a major challenge.

▲
From l'Anse aux Meadows, on a clear day, one can see the Labrador coast across the Strait of Belle Isle. This early warning of visits from their nearest neighbours is likely to have influenced the choice of this site for the first Norse settlement in North America.

Climate

The sea, sea ice, and winds play major roles in the climate of Newfoundland. The Labrador Current is the greatest single influence. Its cold waters delay spring and bring arctic pack ice to surround the Northern Peninsula from December until June or, sometimes, into July. In winter the greater frequency of drier, clearer arctic airstreams towards the northwest of the island results in reduced cloudiness. Summers are short and cool with considerable cloudiness; however, there are occasional warm days near 25o C when the wind is off the land. Average temperatures are -8o C (-4 to -12o C) in February and 12o C (8 to 16o C) in July. Winter temperatures rarely go lower than -20o C; summer temperatures rarely go over 20o C. The frost-free season, which is the growing season, is 100 days. The first frost occurs in late September and the last frost in late June. Lakes and ponds become completely frozen during the first week in December and are completely free of ice by mid-May or a little later. The pond ice is about 75-80 cm thick near St. Anthony.

Wind is a constant feature of the area's weather. The wind is usually northwesterly in the winter and southwesterly in the summer but the area gets considerable wind from the north and northeast, particularly in the spring. Precipitation is about 800-900 mm per year and it occurs on about 100-130 days per year, most of it falling as snow in the winter months. Over the Northern Peninsula there are normally 170-180 days of snow cover (Banfield 1983) reports that, infrequently, there have been as few as 100 days). The ground is snow-covered continuously from January to the end of March. Belle Island, which is in the Strait of Belle Isle only a few kilometres from L'Anse aux Meadows, has at least 2.5 cm of snow on the ground for 186 days per year on average (Potter 1965). I have seen photographs of the Visitors' Centre at L'Anse aux Meadows with nothing showing of it but the peak of the roof, and have skiied to it in winter on a straight line from the road to the Centre because all of the vegetation was under a blanket of snow. In early May, I have visited the replica sod housesbefore the site was officially open, and found snow drifts as much as a metre high inside them.Fog, so typical of a maritime climate, is not as common on the tip of the Northern Peninsula, only occurring about 10 days during the month of June, the month when fog is most frequent.

Dr. Hare (1952), who studied the climate of Newfoundland, said of the tip of the Northern Peninsula that "nowhere else on earth does the Arctic verge drive so far south into the middle latitudes."

In mid July, icebergs can still be plentiful along the East coasts of the Northern Peninsula. From Micky's Hill, you can see the exposed limestone of the harbour islands.

The island of Newfoundland has a fascinating geological history. The island originated with two fragments of continents which collided in the Paleozoic (about 250 million years ago). The Avalon Peninsula is thought to have been part of what is now northwest Africa, and the Northern Peninsula and west coast were and are part of the Appalachian mountain system of North America, which extends south through the eastern United States.

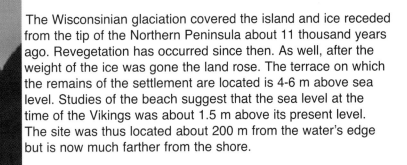

The Wisconsinian glaciation covered the island and ice receded from the tip of the Northern Peninsula about 11 thousand years ago. Revegetation has occurred since then. As well, after the weight of the ice was gone the land rose. The terrace on which the remains of the settlement are located is 4-6 m above sea level. Studies of the beach suggest that the sea level at the time of the Vikings was about 1.5 m above its present level. The site was thus located about 200 m from the water's edge but is now much farther from the shore.

◄ If they sailed this far south, the Norse would surely have seen the similarities of the fjords of the Long Range Mountains (here, Western Brook Pound) to those of Scandinavia and Greenland.
▼

Vegetation

L'Anse aux Meadows is bleak and cold. The vegetation is more like tundra than any other vegetation found on the island. Most of the tip of the Northern Peninsula is less than 60 m in elevation and was flooded by the sea during the Pleistocene glaciation. Soils are very shallow and there are large areas of exposed bedrock. The climate is the chief determining factor of the vegetation in this area. Wind which physically stresses and cools the plants and the cold sea water of the Labrador Current are major influences.

Rocky coastal barrens with low shrubs and a few tuckamores characterize the area. Tuckamores are conifers, mostly balsam fir and white spruce, which grow along the coast and are dwarfed by the constant winds: anything which pokes up above the mass is winter-killed. Tuckamore can be very dense: "You walk in in trousers and come out wearing a kilt". The northern limit of the boreal forest is 8 km south of the Viking site. There are small scattered peatlands throughout the area. A large number of arctic plant species occurs only here on the island. There are also some limestone barrens in the area which have an interesting assemblage of plants, of which several are found here and nowhere else on Earth.

There is no evidence of the introduction of plants by the Vikings in the fossil pollen record as has been found in Greenland. Studies on the pollen fossil record indicated that the vegetation and climate of today and 1000 years ago are very similar. Of the plants we discuss here, the only one which may have been introduced by the Norse is *Urtica*, the stinging nettle.

Griquet harbour from Micky's Hill, late June

The Snorri at anchor in Epaves Bay near the replica sod huts. In the foreground, the red leaf is mostly alpine bearberry; the white is mostly caribou lichen.

Abundant animal life occurred in the area. In the sea were many fish, shellfish, and seals, with which the Vikings would have been familiar. Several varieties of whale were common in the waters around northern Newfoundland: the smallest (and generally the most numerous) of these is the minke, but larger whales such as the humpback, the right, and the fin whale were frequent visitors, and the sperm whale and the blue at least occasionally dropped in. The evidence of the Sagas shows the Norse most likely to take advantage of accidental beachings of whales, more than actively hunting them; but their meetings with the natives of Greenland and of Baffin Island certainly exposed them to whale hunting. The walrus was not common in waters this far south. We know that it was to become a major commercial target for the Greenlanders - walrus ivory was extremely valuable, and walrus hide made some of the best rope available for seagoing ships.

Seabirds nest along the sea cliffs of the Northern Peninsula, and on many of the islands. The flightless great auk (now extinct) was easily captured, and its eggs readily accessible. The gannet is one of the largest of the remaining seabirds - its eggs and the fledglings were relatively easy to gather, though its preference for nesting spots in rock clefts and the like presented considerable hazard. Smaller seabirds would also have been abundant: the murre (or 'turr') and the terns (both Arctic and common terns); and at least three types of gull (kittywake, 'tickle ace' or 'tickle arse' *Rissa tridactyla*; herring gull, *Larus argentatus*;and the largest and most aggressive, the great black-backed gull, 'saddle-back', *Larus marinus*, most likely dominant then as now). There were also numerous shorebirds. On land there were Arctic hare and herds of caribou. The snowshoe hare (called simply 'rabbit' by Newfoundlanders) and the moose are recent introductions both of which the Norse were familiar with from Scandinavia, and both of which they may have hunted on the Labrador. Most populations of animals are now reduced on the Island after 500 years of settlement by Europeans.

◄ A Red Admiral butterfly alights on a clover, Roddickton, early June.

Mating dragonflies, Bell Island (Grey Islands), August.

Black-back chicks are at home in the water from the start. This one swims just off-shore at Dildo Island.

Birds

Black-back gulls (*Larus marinus*) lay their eggs in nests on the ground, relying on camouflage rather than on altitude to protect them. Nests on Dildo Island were placed along the top of a low cliff - not more than five metres above the water. Black-backs are the largest gulls of our area, and dominate other gulls and smaller seabirds. They catch and eat smaller birds (even in flight) as well as eating fish they catch and carrion. Black-backs of our region most commonly catch fish from just below the surface. They will dive, however (their diving behaviour looks remarkably like that of terns), for caplin and herring when those smaller fish are massed for breeding.

Chicks in the grass could be seen easily only when they ➤ moved.

Chicks at Saddle Island, Red Bay, LAB, were huddled against boulders. I chose this group to photograph because the moss on the rock made the chicks much more visible: others I saw were almost impossible to distinguish from the speckled rock.

Adult gannets with young near full size but not yet able to fly. Cape St Mary's, mid August.

The gannet colony at Cape St Mary's is estimated at over five hundred thousand nesting pairs.

An adult gannet near its nesting site at Cape St Mary's on the Avalon peninsula. ➤

◄ Murres 'nest' on cliffside. The eggs are laid on bare rock.

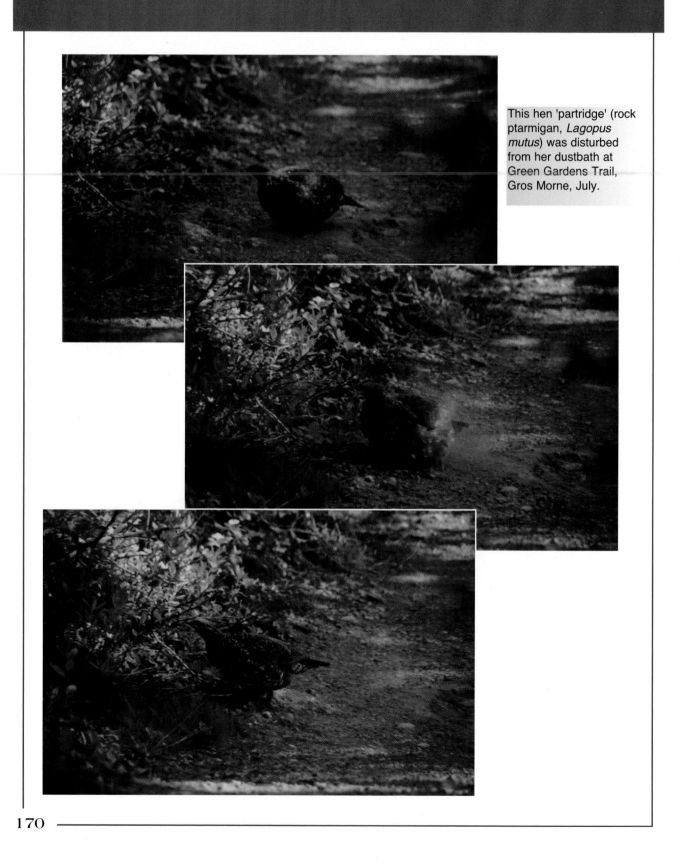

This hen 'partridge' (rock ptarmigan, *Lagopus mutus*) was disturbed from her dustbath at Green Gardens Trail, Gros Morne, July.

Partridges (willow ptarmigan, *Lagopus lagopus*) in a roadside willow near Bide Arm, December.

Puffins *(Fratercula arctica)* nest in very large numbers in the area of Witless Bay (southeast of St. John's). In early summer they feed on caplin and herring which come to this region to spawn. At the other end of the predators' size spectrum, caplin and herring are the principal item on the menu of the whales which make this region their summer feeding ground.

Bird-watching and whale-watching tours are favourite tourist attractions in the St. John's area; but if you want numbers of whales and other sea mammals, and the guarantee of icebergs, the Northern Peninsula is a much better bet.

Puffin nursery, Witless Bay. This site is some sixty metres above sea level, on Gull Island.

Common terns and arctic terns both nest on the same rock ledges. Both will strafe intruders and sound the alarm.

Tern in flight.

From the Sea

A fly fisherman (Lewis Alcock) on Main Brook River. Black Duck Brook at l'Anse aux Meadows was a salmon river, losing its salmon population only when it was dammed to provide water for the Visitors' Centre.

The Atlantic salmon is found now in restricted numbers, and in comparatively few of the many streams and rivers it used to use. This is true on both sides of the Atlantic. Its numbers are small enough that commercial fishing for Atlantic salmon is all but vanished, only farmed fish commercially viable.

There are still enough wild salmon in streams and rivers of northern Newfoundland and southern Labrador to support a healthy sport fishery. When the Vikings were here , salmon as well as cod and many other fish must have been present in great numbers, as they were also when John Cabot first visited the island.

Salt cod dries on an improvised 'flake' - fishnet on sawhorses - at White Cape Harbour, Griquet. The darker the fish, the longer it has been drying.

At low tide, the people of Raleigh gather mussels among the rocks along the shore.

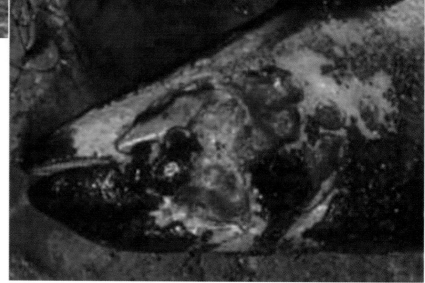

This 'puffin' pig' (harbour porpoise; 'puffing pig') was washed ashore at Bird Cove, already considerably damaged, probably by black-back gulls.

Juvenile harp seals near their breathing hole a few metres from shore at Roddickton in early December. The harbour and the inland portion of Canada Bay are already frozen over, and will stay frozen into April or later.

A juvenile harp seal barks to warn off the intruding photographer. It tolerated my approach to about five metres' distance before acknowledging my presence.

A humpback dives near shore at Great Harbour Deep. This whale's right tail fluke has been sheared off - the clean cut and good healing suggest a ship's propeller as the culprit. This photo series was taken in mid July, during the caplin run.

Land Mammals

A caribou bull in his breeding form in October. His cows are less conspicuous, but also bear short antlers.Adult caribou generally lose their antlers in late winter.

The winter has taken a toll: you can easily count the ribs of the largest cow here. Caribou are easiest to find in spring. They keep to low ground, where the snow melts first. As spring and summer progress they will move to higher ground, descending generally in late fall as snow cover deepens.

Two adult cow caribou and a juvenile in October near a quarry close to the former St. Anthony airport. They are a part of the 'harem' of the handsome bull opposite. Freshwater streams and shallow ponds are already frozen.

An adult grey fox in late July near Stuckless Pond in Gros Morne Park. Urbanites in North America would not consider a fox edible; but foxes have been on the menu for aboriginal people, and for the European settlers of this region, for a very long time. "Hunger makes the best sauce." In winter, and in particular in early spring when the food stored for winter was getting down to its last, fox must have been a welcome addition to the larder.

▲ Th e snowshoe hare (*Lepus americanus*) seen here is the 'rabbit' of modern Newfoundland, a fairly recent introduction to the island. The Arctic hare, a larger animal, has been present at least since the last major glaciation ended 11,000 years ago. It is now found mostly at higher elevations where the snowshoe hare is less well equipped to cope. This was taken at Cow Head, Gros Morne National Park.

A young bull moose goes 'down on his knucks' to graze on coltsfoot (*Tussilago farfara*) in late May.

He was grazing at the foot of a steep road-side slope, and continued contentedly grazing until he was less than ten metres away from me. At that point I decided to make my way back to my car.

Young bull moose grazing on coltsfoot.

◄ A young cow moose in open woods along Rte 430, the Viking Trail, outside St. Anthony. The white triangular 'vulvar patch' is a very common feature of cow moose.

Even in early spring, ► bulls one year old or older will show at least the buds of antlers.

Distribution Table

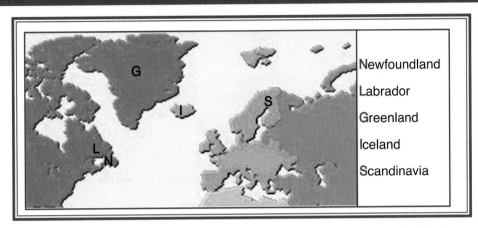

Newfoundland

Labrador

Greenland

Iceland

Scandinavia

Many of the plants below have similar species in Scandinavia but not necessarily the same species.

Species	Common Name	Distribution
Abies balsamea	balsam fir	NL
Actaea rubra	actea	NL
Alnus crispa	alder	NLGIS
[A. rugosa - absent from Northern Penninsula]		
Amelanchier bartramiana	chuckley pear	NL
Andromeda glaucophylla	bog rosemary	NLG
Angelica		
A. atropurpurea	angelica	NL
A. archangelica	alexanders	NLGS
Arctostaphylos		
A. alpina	alpine bearberry	NLGS
A. rubra,	red bearberry	N
A. uva-ursi	evergreen bearberry	NLGIS
Aronia prunifolia	purple chokeberry	N
Atriplex glabriuscula	smooth orache	NLGS
Chamaedaphne calyculata	leatherleaf	NLS

Clintonia borealis	clintonia	NL
Cornus		
C. canadensis	bunchberry, crackerberry	NLG
C. suecica	Swedish bunchberry	NLGIS
Empetrum		
E. atropurpureum	purple crowberry	NL
E. eamesii	pink crowberry	NL
E. nigrum	blackberry	NLGIS
Epigaea repens	trailing arbutus	N
Epilobium angustifolium	fireweed	NLGS
Fragaria		
F. virginiana	common strawberry	NL
F. vesca	wood strawberry	NS
Gaultheria hispidula capillaire	snowberry	NL
Geum rivale	purple avens	NLS
Heracleum maximum	cow parsnip	NL
Iris versicolor	iris	NL
Juniperus		
J.communis	juniper	NLGIS
J. horizontalis	trailing juniper	N
Kalmia		
K. angustifolia	sheep laurel, lambkill	NL
K. polifolia	bog laurel/pale laurel	NL
Larix laricina	larch	NL
Latyhrus		
L. maritima	beach pea	NLGS
L. palustris	vetchling	NLS
[Ledum see Rhododendron]		
Ligusticum scothicum	scotch lovage	NLGS

Mertensia maritima	oysterleaf	NLGS
Moneses uniflora	one-flowered wintergreen	NLS
Monotropa uniflora	Indian pipe	NL
Myrica	gale, sweet gale	NLS
Picea		
P. glauca	white spruce	NL
P. mariana	black spruce	NL
Plantago maritima	beach plantain	NLGS
Polygonum viviparum	alpine smartweed	NLS
Potentilla		
P. anserina	silverweed	NLGIS
P. fruticosa	shrubby cinquefoil	NLS
P. norvegica	rough cinquefoil	NLG*IS
P. palustris	marsh cinquefoil	NLGIS
P. pulchella	Burnt Cape cinquefoil	NLGS
= P. usticapensis (after Scoggan))		
P. tridentata	three-toothed cinquefoil	NLG
Prunus pennsylvanica	pin cherry	NL
Pyrola		
P. asarifolia	pink pyrola	N
P. elliptica	white pyrola	N
P. minor	lesser pyrola	NLGIS
P. secunda	one-sided pyrola	NLGIS
Rhamnus alnifolia	buckthorn	N
Rhododendron		
R. groenlandicum	Labrador tea	NLG
R. lapponicum	Lapland rosebay	NLGS
R. canadense	rhodora	N
Ribes		
R. lacustre	bristly black currant	NL
R. hirtellum	gooseberry	N
R. glandulosum	skunk currant	NL
R. triste	swampy red currant	NL

* indicates an introduced species.

Rosa   rose
none reported on Northern Peninsula (nitida not NP - Ryan 97) and virginiana

Rubus
    R. acaulis   raspberry; dewberry   N
        (similar spp. from Scandinavia)
    R. chamaemorus   bakeapple, cloudberry   NLGS
    R. idaeus   common raspberry   NLS
    R. paracaulis   arctic plumboy   NLS
    R. pubescens   plumboy, dewberry   N

Salix
    S. argyrocarpon   silverleaf willow   NL
    S. brachycarpa   Canadian willow   NL
    S. cardifolia   ungava willow   NL
    S. discolor   pussy willow   NL
    S. glauca   grey willow   NL
    S. reticulata   netvein dwarf willow   NL
    S. uva-ursi   bearberry dwarf willow   NLG
    S. vestita   Waghorn's willow   N

Sedum rosea   roseroot   NLS

Shepherdia canadensis   soapberry   N

Smilacina stellata   starry false Solomon's seal   NL

Sorbus
    S. decora   dogberry, mountain ash, rowan   NL
    S. decora var. groenlandica northern dogberry   NLG
    S. americana   american dogberry   NL

Streptopus
    S. amplexifolius   twisted stalk   NLG
    S. roseus   rose twisted stalk   NL

Tussilago farfara   coltsfoot   NS

Urtica dioica   *stinging nettle*   NS

Vaccinium
    V. itis-idaea   partridgeberry   NLGIS
        lingonberry (Eur.), mountain cranberry (US)]
    V. oxycoccos   small cranberry; marshberry   NLGS
    V. macrocarpon   large cranberry   N

blueberry/bilberry		
V. angustifolium	blueberry	NL
V. boreale	Newfoundland dwarf blueberry	NL
V. ovalifolium	oval-leaved bilberry	NL
V. uliginosum	tundra bilberry	NLGIS
Viburnum		
V. cassinoides	northern wild raisin	N
V. edule	squashberry	NL
V. trilobum	high-bush cranberry	N

Bibliography

Banfield, C.E., *"Climate" in South* 1983.

Burzynski, Michael, *Gros Morne National Park*, St. John's 1999.

Collins, Michael, *Plants and Wildflowers of Newfoundland*, St. John's 1994.

Draskóy, George F. et al., *The Great Northern Peninsula: an archaeological and geological history*, St. John's 1971.

Fleurbec *Plantes sauvages comestibles*, Groupe Fleurbec 1981.

Fleurbec *Plantes sauvages au menu (guide culinaire),* Groupe Fleurbec 1981.

Gardon, Anne, *The Wild Food Gourmet: fresh and savory food from nature,* Willowdale, ON 1998.

Garnett, Blanche Pownell, *A Taste of the Wild,* Toronto 1975.

Green, Ivan J., *A Collection of Vascular Plants of Insular Newfoundland,* St. John's 1984.

Lacey, Laurie *Micmac Medicines,* Halifax 1993.

Meades, Susan J. "The Barrens: Heathlands of Newfoundland" *Wildflower* 9 (1) Winter 1993 pp. 32-5.
    This issue of Wildflower is entirely devoted to Newfoundland, and contains many articles of interest.

Newfoundland and Labrador Women's Institutes, *Favourite WI Berry Recipes*, St. John's 1997.

Peterson, Lee Allen et al., *Edible Wild Plants,* Boston/New York 1977.

Peterson, Roger Tory and Margaret McKenny, *Wildflowers Northeastern/Northcentral North America*, New York 1968/1996.

Ryan, A. Glen, *Native Trees and Shrubs of Newfoundland and Labrador,* St. John's 1995.

Scoggan, H.G, *The Flora of Canada, National Museums of Canada*, Ottawa. 4 vols. 1978.

South, G. Robin, *Biogeography and Ecology of the Island of Newfoundland.* Dr. W. Junk Publishers, The Hague 1983.

Strickler, Dee, *Forest Wildflowers: Showy Wildflowers of the Woods, Mountains and Forests of the Northern Rocky Mountain States,* Billings, Montana 1988.

Titford, Bill and June, *A Traveller's Guide to Wild Flowers of Newfoundland,* Canada, St. John's 1995.

Turner, Nancy J. and Adam F. Szczawinski, *Edible Wild Fruits and Nuts of Canada* National Museum of Natural Science n.d.

Tuck, James A., *Ancient People of Port au Choix* St. John's 1976.